Books Speaking to Books

BOOKS SPEAKING TO BOOKS

A Contextual Approach to
American Fiction

by William T. Stafford

The University of North Carolina Press

Chapel Hill

For Fran—
and our three daughters,
Lindy, Jocy, Katy

© 1981 The University of North Carolina Press
All rights reserved
Manufactured in the United States of America
Library of Congress Cataloging in Publication Data

Stafford, William T
Books speaking to books.

Includes bibliographical references and index.
CONTENTS: Introduction: listening.—A whale, an heir-
ess, and a southern demigod: three symbolic Americas.—
Benjy Compson, Jake Barnes, and Nick Carraway: replica-
tion in three "innocent" American narrators of the
1920s.—[etc.]
1. American fiction—History and criticism—
Addresses, essays, lectures. 2. Influence (Literary,
artistic, etc.)—Addresses, essays, lectures.
I. Title.
PS371.S68   813'.009   80-25892
ISBN 0-8078-1469-5

Contents

Acknowledgments
vii

1. Introduction: Listening
3

2. A Whale, an Heiress, and a Southern Demigod:
Three Symbolic Americas
11

3. Benjy Compson, Jake Barnes, and Nick Carraway:
Replication in Three "Innocent" American
Narrators of the 1920s
27

4. The Obverse Relation:
Some Western Flights Eastward
(in Literature and Film)
51

5. The Black/White Continuum:
Some Recent Examples in Bellow, Malamud, and Updike
71

6. Three Applications
103

Truth's Ragged Edges:
Melville's Loyalties in *Billy Budd*—
The Commitment of Form in the Digressions
105

"The Birthplace": James's Fable for Critics?
114

Faulkner's Revolt against the 1920s:
Parody and Transcendence, Continuation and Innovation
119

7. Afterword: "Knower, Doer, and Sayer"—
The James Family View of Emerson
127

Notes
151

Index
161

Acknowledgments

THE IMPISH TEMPTATION to deny any debts to the scores of students I have known over the years must, I suppose, be resisted. Many of them have been exposed to much of what has been written in this collection, and more than a few of them have responded to those essays in ways that were surely helpful. The equally impish impulse to deny any support from my wife and daughters, to lament, say, their too infrequent visits to mom or grandmother, must also be resisted. In truth, theirs has been a loving and tolerant accommodation to my many necessary absences, when no farther than to my office on weekends or week nights or when of much longer duration and of distance. Students and family both have legitimate demands of their own. What I gained from them is in all likelihood more than they gained from me. I owe them all much, and all, I am sure, know it.

I am of course also in debt to many present and former colleagues here at Purdue: to the chairman of my department, Jacob H. Adler, for his consistent support of my scholarly activities; to Robert L. Ringel, the dean of my school, and Arthur G. Hansen, president of Purdue, for granting me the sabbatical semester that allowed me unfettered time to revise and extend several of the essays in this collection; to Margaret Church, my coeditor of *Modern Fiction Studies*, who on more than one occasion has assumed the responsibilities of full editorship to free me for these interests of my own; to Leslie Field, for sharing with me his broad knowledge of Jewish-American writers; to Leonard Neufeldt, for steering me toward some of the best recent scholarship on Emerson; to Joe Palmer, for his only sometimes scintillating views of current movies; to William Bache, whose comments on the links often have as much to do with critical stances as they do with golf ones; to Martin Light, simply for frequent, good, provocative talk about American fiction; and to those present and former *MFS* editorial assistants Carla Cooper, John Guzlowski, Bonnie Eddy, and Martin Rapisarda, off whom I so often (and for me so fruitfully) bounced many of the ideas in these essays. Martin Rapisarda deserves special thanks for his meticulous help in proofreading no less than for his general good humor, patience, and wit. I also appreciate the good work done by my various typists—Cherylynn Knott, John Paschke, and Shirley Thompson, all members of the Purdue English department secretarial staff.

The two scholars to whom I owe the most in helping me shape the final form of the essays in this collection are C. Hugh Holman, of The University of North Carolina at Chapel Hill, and Maurice Beebe, editor of the *Journal of Modern Literature*, at Temple University. That they are both dear friends of long standing—Beebe, in fact, was a colleague here at Purdue and, during its first fourteen years, editor of *Modern Fiction Studies*—in no way forestalled their candid and stringent suggestions for improving these essays. As is often the case with suggestions from close friends, some I was happy to follow and some I did not. The responsibility, at any rate, is ultimately mine, not theirs. But both must know, like students and family, like colleagues and staff, that my appreciation is sincere, my debts to them all, although of varying degrees, heartfelt and extensive.

I wish also to thank those editors and publishers who allowed me to reprint material that first appeared in their respective journals: Bernard Oldsey, editor of *College Literature*, wherein "A Whale, an Heiress, and a Southern Demigod" first appeared (1 [Spring 1974]: 100–112); Ray Browne, editor of the *Journal of Popular Culture*, wherein a brief part of "The Obverse Relation" first appeared (8 [Fall 1974]: 320–27); and Edwin H. Cady, editor of *American Literature*, wherein a radically different version of "'Knower, Doer, and Sayer'" first appeared (24 [January 1953]: 431–61) under the title "Emerson and the James Family" and copyrighted 1953 by Duke University Press.

I would be remiss not also to mention here the various

courtesies and above all the promptness with which Malcolm
Call, the former editor-in-chief of The University of North
Carolina Press, and his staff have facilitated the production
of my book.

Last, but certainly not least, is my ineffable gratitude to
R. A. M. for untold contributions to the production of my
book in its final stages.

Books Speaking to Books

ONE

Introduction

Listening

I HAVE BEEN listening to books speak to books for many years. They have spoken in various voices, and I have heard them while in various moods. This collection of essays represents some of the sometimes eloquent, sometimes outrageous things that I have heard. All readers, I would suppose, listen to books speak to books. Every reader, I would further suppose, is a very selective listener, inevitably subjective, inevitably conditioned by that concomitant of circumstance that makes each of us what he is. One may well, moreover, have been listening to books speak to books without quite knowing he was doing so. In fact, he may have been a practiced eavesdropper to this kind of imagined literary conversation without quite knowing he was one. Such, at any rate, was my own experience.

The earliest-written essay in this collection, printed here as an afterword, "'Knower, Doer, and Sayer': The James Family View of Emerson," was originally a totally un-self-conscious act in this regard. It happened to me more than I to it. First conceived as a paper for a seminar I was taking on Emerson, it had, during its gestation period, nothing more theoretically "aware" in support of its methodology than the intrinsic neatness of its self-circumscribed boundaries: three illustrious members of a single illustrious family—Henry, William, and their father, the elder Henry James—on the subject of Ralph Waldo Emerson. When I first began listening to members of the James family on the subject of Emerson, I of course had little knowledge of what it was that I would hear. The more I heard, however, the more symmetrical was the orchestration that began to emerge. It was not until years later that I began to wonder to what extent the beautifully intricate pattern that did emerge was the result of selective hearing rather than of something inherent in the voices themselves. Had I, in short, created the pattern or was it always there, simply waiting to be heard? I readdress this issue at the end of this volume, listening again, as it were, to what I originally heard, but with, I would hope, somewhat more sensitive ears—and perhaps even a somewhat more articulate voice to report what I am now hearing. What is given there is thus both the earliest and the most recent of these otherwise generally chronologically arranged excursions. I am collecting it as an afterword in part because its subject matter differs—the other essays are all centrally concerned with fiction—in part because it most clearly expands my methodology even as it literally represents its beginnings. Some readers may well wish to begin the collection with it.

The first essay in this book, on Melville's *Moby-Dick*, James's *The Wings of the Dove*, and Faulkner's *Absalom, Absalom!*, was a much more methodical and self-conscious affair than the Emerson/James family study. It too, however, had a classroom gestation, but in this instance from the point of view of the teacher rather than that of the student. The class was an honors seminar for underclass students with the title "The Many Americas of Melville, James, and Faulkner" and had for its required reading early, middle, and late novels by each of these writers: an early "travel" novel by each (*Typee, The American, As I Lay Dying*), a late "initiation" book by each (*Billy Budd, What Maisie Knew, The Reivers*), and a great middle "tragedy" by each (the three novels first mentioned in this paragraph). The "plan" for the class was for these novels to be read and discussed rapidly in the order given. Each student was then to read on his own an additional novel by each of these writers and present a paper in which he or she, through some symbolic, thematic, or tactical link, searched for a perspective not readily apparent without the special context provided through the ties the student established. The students were instructed to pay no attention to possible "source" studies. The assignment was simply to discover whether a clearly defined and limited context of three novels by three of America's most eminent novelists rendered insights of a kind possibly not apparent in any other way.

I believed that they would, and because at that time I also believed that teachers themselves should at least occasionally attempt that which they ask of their students—although not giving up the equally strong conviction that a teacher should never flinch from asking students questions to which he or she does not know the "answer"—I nevertheless in this instance set about attempting to show the class what it was that I wanted it to attempt. "A Whale, an Heiress, and a Southern Demigod: Three Symbolic Americas" was the result. And it was this relatively brief, informal, perhaps even somewhat facetious class exercise that was the true germ of the essays that followed, not the much earlier written "'Knower, Doer, and Sayer.'"

Although in conception and indeed in execution my "Three Symbolic Americas" was a "fun" exercise, I took it (or at least its methodology) with deadly seriousness. For the long, heavily documented essay that followed on Benjy Compson, Jake Barnes, and Nick Carraway was flying full in the face of three of the most various and most explicated American novels of the twentieth century, Faulkner's *The Sound and the Fury*, Hemingway's *The Sun Also Rises*, and Fitzgerald's *The Great Gatsby*. Here, in short, was a test case par excellence. Although realizing that my "reading" of each novel was in no way startlingly new, I was able to see some fresh implications in each of them through my reflexive focus on the subject and the methodology of innocent narrators in the limited, replicated context of three American novels of the 1920s.

Never able, however, to sustain high seriousness for very long, I next expanded my contextual approach to six works, unlike my previous limit to sets of three, and I adventured, moreover, into a mixture of other genres, comparing James's *The American* with Dennis Hopper's film *Easy Rider* in one subset, Hemingway's supposedly nonfictional *Green Hills of Africa* with Twain's novel *A Connecticut Yankee in King Arthur's Court* in another, and two Italian-made films, Bernardo Bertolucci's *Last Tango in Paris* and Sergio Leone's *Once upon a Time in the West* in a third. If one kind of test of my contextual methodology had been represented by the previous essay, "Three 'Innocent' American Narrators of the 1920s," a quite different kind was represented by "The Obverse Relation: Some Western Flights Eastward (in Literature and Film)." It was different not only in that it edged over into the area of so-called popular culture (and in its consequent mixture of lowbrow and highbrow). It was also different in that it used a much looser concept of context than had any of the previous essays. In its diversity of genres, moreover, it opened up questions of how the effects of one genre might affect those of another when placed within a single context. Finally, among the essays in this book, it was simply the most fun to write.

The last of my major chapters, "The Black/White Continuum: Some Recent Examples in Bellow, Malamud, and Updike," is possibly the most tightly controlled, self-conscious exemplum of my method in this book. Its look at the black/

white pairs in *Mr. Sammler's Planet, The Tenants*, and *Rabbit Redux* is additionally marked by the proximity of the publication dates of the three novels (all during 1970 or 1971), by the roughly analogous position each novel holds in the canon of each of its authors, and by the collective reaction that all three authors had to a single cultural phenomenon, life in America during the late 1960s. With the single exception of the James family, it is, insofar as I know, the only example of a context so readily apparent that it has been treated as such by other critics, most of whom are referred to in the essay itself. Even so, it is not an isolated case. In fact, it has more than specious ties to the germinal essay for this collection, "Three Symbolic Americas," for it was while writing that essay that the idea for this one first came to me, as I there remarked. More significantly, perhaps, one of the elements revealed in that early context was a prophetic, "contemporary" quality in those early novels, whereas a complementary old, familiar, quite conventional element emerges in the context of these three most recent novels. The two essays thus pair nicely.

The last essay in this book also has its ties to "Three Symbolic Americas." My three examples there are works of fiction by the same three eminent novelists represented in the earlier essay, Melville, Henry James, and Faulkner. More important, however, are the attempts there to demonstrate some widely diversified, albeit discrete, applications of some of the concepts of context demonstrated in the previous chapters. Although I give my rationale for those diverse applications in a prefatory note to those three final essays, I would here remark that Melville's *Billy Budd*, James's "The Birthplace," and three early novels by Faulkner (*The Sound and the Fury, As I Lay Dying*, and *Light in August*) could not finally have been read as they are had they not had back of those readings some such concepts of context as previously revealed. The *Billy Budd* example could be described as a *constrictive* contextual analysis; "The Birthplace," as an *expansive* one; the Faulkner novels, as an *amalgam* of the two.

The highly personal tone of these introductory remarks is a fully self-conscious result of my firmly held conviction that literary criticism is a very subjective activity. Whatever the variety of poses to the contrary, that which is finally demonstrated is a single and therefore restrictive critical reaction to a literary work. What one sees in that analysis (or what one hears, to revert to my introductory trope) may or may not be enlightening or acceptable or indeed even possible for some of one's audience, and if this last *is* the case— who among us has not listened to critics he could not finally hear?—one always has the simple option of turning away.

Still, it is not critical anarchy that I am advocating, nor is it pure subjectivism. When asked for his reaction to some extreme interpretations of "Stopping by Woods," Robert Frost is said to have responded that "the poet is entitled to whatever the reader can find in his poem" (a statement I have always "heard" to be saying, "Whatever anyone gets out of this poem *I* put there"). That should be a sufficient reminder of the pitfalls of that path. After all, the work itself, the text, is still the supreme thing, and almost all criticism is a form of parasitism (as I somehow hear James saying in "The Birthplace"). Even so, I am almost always willing to give an initial critical hearing to any critical discourse as long as I am not restricted by a concomitant demand to hear it as the *only* approach to a given literary subject. No such critical codicil is therefore intended or implied in this collection of essays. At the same time I should also confess that I have long professed also to believe that the only ultimate criterion to apply to literary criticism is what Henry James called, in another connection, "a very obvious truth": to wit, "the deepest quality of a work of art will always be the quality of the mind that produced it." That terrifying dictum, which I have so often applied to the criticism of others, I recognize somewhat diffidently, cannot be irrelevant to my own.

This simple and avowedly personal critical stance is, of course, more to be tested in its application (in the essays that follow) than in this prefatory formulation. Its possible worth must rest there, not here. What is *here*, in fact, clearly first came from *there*. I would thus be hard put were I required to codify that stance without reference to the literature that engendered it. Still, it has been suggested to me that some critical theorists as disparate in time and point of view as James Baird in his *Ishmael* (1956) and Harold Bloom in his *The Anxiety of Influence* (1973) or his *A Map of Misreading* (1975) might well be useful to me were I to attempt some more extensive theoretical codification of my views. Well, perhaps. In the meantime I was exposed to the opening and closing chapters of Wayne C. Booth's recent *Critical Under-standing: The Powers and Limits of Pluralism* (Chicago: University of Chicago Press, 1980). What I found there struck me as covering with such meticulous thoroughness the essential elements of the so-called critical act (or acts) that I seriously wondered whether anything else ever needed to be said on the subject. All this, let me admit with some shame, was without having read those portions of Booth's book that are devoted to application—thus audaciously violating his first cardinal principle in his appended "A Hippocratic Oath for the Pluralist": "I will publish nothing, favorable or unfavorable, about books or articles I have not read through at least once." I here justify the violation in small part simply because I do not normally think of myself as a pluralist. (I am in fact quite "monistic" in my support of what I understand Booth's "pluralism" to be!) More seriously, it was Booth's corroborating voice of critical tolerance that I found most appealing. What might have happened to that voice in application I obviously cannot say. What I can say, however (and this is my only rationale for this extended reference to Booth's book), is that it is the general critical stance of *Critical Understanding* that I would most like to think I have approached, well aware though I am, of the gargantuan disparities between that ambitious, erudite work and this much more modest one.

A final word remains to be said about the widely disparate tones of the various essays in this book. This variety in part results from the compositional history of each essay, in part from design. The opening and closing essays were published in scholarly journals soon after they were written. The first is given in a slightly different form; the latter is here revised in a much more radical way. A small part of "The Obverse Relation" was also previously published. All of the remaining essays, with the exception of "The Black/White Continuum," have been presented as lectures before a variety of audiences for a variety of reasons in a variety of places, both here and abroad. A final decision, however, was to make no attempt to achieve any uniformity of tone. Books speak to books, I have now known for a long time, in a multiplicity of voices.

TWO

A Whale, an Heiress, and a Southern Demigod

Three Symbolic Americas

THE "AMERICANNESS" OF the American novel is no longer a hotly debated topic. Examples are too ubiquitous, in poetry, drama, biography, chronicle, and essay, no less than in fiction, and in our earliest literature no less than in our most recent. It is now almost sixty years since D. H. Lawrence proclaimed (in his *Studies in Classic American Literature* in 1923) that "the hour" was "struck," that "Americans shall be American," that indeed, as he was to contend, they always had been, perhaps more covertly ("under the American bushes") than overtly, but everywhere compulsively, quintessentially *there*. The resulting critical commonplace is that an American-rendered character, idea, situation, embodiment is somehow thereby a rendition of the "true" American experience.

Thus it is no great critical surprise that we now view one of our very earliest novels, Charles Brockden Brown's *Arthur Mervyn* (1799–1800), as a portrayal of a generic American. When young Arthur throws over the fair-haired young virgin who loves him to marry the rich, dark, much older, divorced and/or widowed European Jewess Ascha Fielding, it may be seen as a generic act. Mervin's initial poverty thus "keys" the theme of rags to riches. His bucolic background signals a revolt from the village. His desire to get ahead in essence is get-up-and-go. The polarized nature of his two lady loves (one fair and one dark) reflects racial schizophrenia. His sly opportunism in selecting the rich and seductive mama-figure and rejecting the poor, blonde virgin is the American conflict between Jew and goy, between Europe and America, between mother and daughter.

The poor, domestic, womanless bliss enjoyed by Cooper's Natty Bumppo and Chingachgook in the Leatherstocking Tales is seen (by Leslie Fiedler and others) as representing American puritanical fear of woman—and its adolescent obverse, flight from the city to the woods with a male companion, preferably with one of a darker race (most often Indian or Negro) to assuage the guilt of American oppression and bigotry. In part, Arthur Dimmesdale and Hester Prynne (of Hawthorne's *The Scarlet Letter*) are an intricate representation of this same trait, that is, an affirmation of and a simultaneous rebellion against American Puritanism.

Henry David Thoreau's microcosmic mini-retreat to Walden Pond clearly rehearses the recurring American retreat

from the woman-dominated, bustling hub-bub of village life
to the wholesome solitude and individualized irresponsibility
of a kind of anarchism close to nature, that is, to "life in the
woods," Thoreau's own subtitle. Rip Van Winkle's twenty-
year sleep might well be the same. Huckleberry Finn's de-
termination not to be "sivilized" and to "light out for the
Territory" is certainly in part a response to the same American impulse characterized by Cooper a half-century earlier,
and Huck's relationship with Nigger Jim reworks a theme
embodied in Natty's ties to Chingachgook.

Modern examples are no less numerous, from Dreiser's *An
American Tragedy* (seen as "Death in the Woods") to Fitzgerald's *The Great Gatsby* (seen as *the* American dream).
Thomas Wolfe's autobiographical protagonist is no less meant
to be *the* American than is Whitman's personified *I* in *Song
of Myself.* And nothing less inclusive than *U.S.A.* is the title
of John Dos Passos's most ambitious work.

Recent American fiction is no exception. J. D. Salinger's
Holden Caulfield (of *The Catcher in the Rye*) is no less the all-
American boy than is Huck Finn—or Horatio Alger. Saul
Bellow's *Henderson the Rain King* and John Barth's *The Sot-
Weed Factor* both depict what are clearly meant to be American types. Philip Roth's *Portnoy's Complaint* presents precisely the complaint Philip Wylie named "Momism" in his
Generation of Vipers way back in 1944. There is no surprise
or novelty, therefore, in finding generic conceptions in such
obviously named characters as Captain America and Billy
the Kid in Dennis Hopper's highly praised and popular film
Easy Rider (1969). But perhaps there is some surprise in
seeing ancient racial formulas reappearing with such regu-
larity in such recent and otherwise innovative novels as Bellow's *Mr. Sammler's Planet*, Malamud's *The Tenants*, and
Updike's *Rabbit Redux*—at least insofar as all three appear
to be repeating in their black/white pairs of characters mere
variations on the Huck-Jim relationship. (This last is the
specific subject of a later essay.)

My subject here, however, is three earlier American novelists, more specifically, three American novels, one each by
Herman Melville, Henry James, and William Faulkner. All
three writers produced an extensive corpus; all three were
imaginative innovators; all three have been enormously in-
fluential. Their renditions of symbolic Americas, of course,

are not restricted to the three novels to be examined here in some detail: *Moby-Dick*, *The Wings of the Dove*, and *Absalom, Absalom!* Being in the American tradition—indeed, in some seminal ways, creators of it—their works are everywhere illustrative of that larger and more pervasive context already suggested.

To look at these novels in this highly restricted way is, to be sure, to distort them. Yet I do not believe I am ultimately playing them false. They are among the best novels by these three writers precisely because of the multiplicity of meanings they reveal, precisely because among that multiplicity of meanings there is one complex of configurations that defines their shared homeland and thus links them together— even as it reveals their disparate artistic visions.

Moby Dick as America

One way to view the great whale hunt of *Moby-Dick* is to view the gathering of the crew for the *Pequod*, their odyssey halfway around the world, and their ultimate confrontation with and destruction by the great white whale as simply their failed attempt to come to terms with, their failure to make intelligible, a magnificently *natural* phenomenon. The phenomenon as symbol, let us view as Moby Dick; the phenomenon as fact, let us view as an "idea" of "America."

For the people who settled it the American continent was never mere land. It was also always an idea: the New Jerusalem, the second Garden of Eden, the home of the free and the land of the brave. But it was a wilderness too, a terrifyingly gothic horror, a "dark and bloody ground," a landscape of savage and primitive unintelligibility. If it was the home of towering mountains and majestic plains, it was also the home of the Dakota badlands and the Okefenokee swamps.

It is precisely this ambivalence about the land (Is it to be possessed and changed, or is it to be preserved, revered, and held sacred?) that characterizes Melville's first complex rendition of the whale. The first detailed description of the quarry occurs in chapter 41, in which we are told about his "peculiar snow-white wrinkled forehead, and a high, pyramidical white hump." Melville adds that "these were his prominent features; the tokens whereby, even in the limitless, unchartered seas, he reveals his identity, at a long distance, to those who knew him." Then he says: "The rest of his body was so streaked, and spotted, and marbled with the same shrouded hue, that, in the end, he had gained his distinctive appellation of the White Whale; a name, indeed, literally justified by his vivid aspect, when seen gliding at high noon through a dark blue sea, leaving a milky-way wake of creamy foam, all spangled with golden gleamings."

The more famous chapter that follows, "The Whiteness of the Whale," has as its penultimate line this unequivocal assertion: "And of all these things the Albino whale was the symbol." The well-known discussion in that chapter includes an elaborate listing of the ambiguous, contradictory, and ultimately mystifying ways that we react to whiteness. The list is too well known to repeat here, but Melville's questioning summing-up perhaps is not. For "not yet," he writes, "have we solved the incantation of this whiteness, and learned why it appeals with such power to the soul; and more strange and far more portentous—why . . . it is at once the most meaning symbol of spiritual things, nay, the very veil of the Christian's Deity; and yet should be as it is, the intensifying agent in things the most appalling to mankind."

What the white whale in fact means is, of course, the central burden of the entire book, even as its representation of what America means is the burden of this particular exegesis. A brilliant analysis made by James Dean Young in an article called "The Nine Gams of the *Pequod*" (published in *American Literature* 25 [1954]: 449–63) may provide one answer to both. Young demonstrates how the nine gams of the *Pequod*—a gam is a whaler's name for a meeting at sea with another whaler—were a symbolic and structural device for narrowing and refining the definition of the true nature of the *Pequod*'s quest. The internal evidence justifying his approach is considerable: as we have Ahab asking each ship the same question ("Hast thou seen the white whale?") and as each ship is symbolically its own world as the *Pequod* itself so clearly and unmistakably is, we have one basis for discovering what *its* view is by contrasting it to that of nine other worlds.

Instead of asking "Hast thou seen the white whale?" we can ask something roughly formulated to say, "What do you consider the American continent, the American experience, to be?"

The *Pequod*'s first three gams are with the *Albatross* (chapter 52), the *Town-Ho* (chapter 54), and the *Jeroboam* (chapter 71). In this first series of meetings no articulated, literal communication transpires; meaning here comes through signs, symbols, and action—portentous, mystifying, and suggestive, but perhaps all the more meaningful by virtue of the indirection required. The *Albatross*, for example, is met in a rough sea; the trumpet, which its captain raises to his mouth through which to speak, unaccountably falls from his hand into the sea. The ship thus sails silently by. One suggestion here is the impossibility of communication with a world maniacally ruled (as the *Pequod* is by Ahab) when the winds of heaven are astir unless extraordinary means are employed. Communication is possible in the second gam, with the *Town-Ho*, but it comes only to the crew, not Ahab, who never hears it; we hear it only as retold by Ishmael years later in Peru. The crew of the *Town-Ho* communicates only with Tashtego, who inadvertently relates it (in his sleep) to the crew of the *Pequod*, but not to Ahab or his mates. He tells a strange, wonderous tale of how Moby Dick was the instrument of divine justice in destroying an evil mate named Radney, who had been inhumanly cruel to a godlike, handsome young sailor named Steelkilt. The possibility of America being the instrument of God and known as such to its people, if not to its leaders (Ahab and the mates), must be clear enough. In the third gam, the meeting with the *Jeroboam*, we have another equation between Moby Dick and God, but this time a sort of diabolical one as the ship is in control of the madman Gabriel, an epidemic is loose on board, and the view of Moby Dick (read America?) is that it will destroy those who dare assail its enigmatic divinity. We thus see here in these first three gams warnings and prophecies, unmistakable predictions of doom, no communication with those in authority, and, perhaps, finally, views of America as paradoxically both benign and diabolical.

The method of the second triad of gams is much more direct and straightforward, and the clearcut nationalistic concept of these three gams is persuasive evidence of the "Americanism" embodied in *Moby-Dick*. For the gams with the *Jungfrau* (chapter 81), the *Rose Bud* (chapter 91), and the *Samuel*

Enderby (chapter 100) are clearly meant to be, respectively, German, French, and British contrasts to and attitudes about the American quest for the whale. The innocence of the Germans and the superficial inexperience of the French are obvious enough as intelligible attitudes toward the whale, even if unacceptable ones to the *Pequod*. But the British perspective deserves a little more attention, for the sensible Captain Boomer of the *Samuel Enderby*, like Ahab, has grappled with Moby Dick and lost a limb. Boomer, however, having sighted the whale a second time, was not about to attack again. "Ain't one limb enough?" he shouts—a totally common-sensical response, even if unacceptable to Ahab. For the American captain of the *Pequod*, Boomer's view is mere supercilious facetiousness. But for us his is a totally understandable response, especially as it so vividly contrasts with what we view as the compulsive monomania of Ahab—a monomania, we are beginning to see with more and more clarity, Melville perceptively conceives of as uniquely American.

The last three gams, those with the *Bachelor*, the *Rachel*, and the *Delight* (chapters 115, 128, and 131, respectively), increase the pace, race toward the climax, and give us (through the technique of exclusion) our final definition of the *Pequod* before its encounter with and destruction by the great white whale. All three of these ships are significantly American and thus provide alternative ways of looking at the whale even as their conditions become additional symbolic comments about the America they symbolically embody. Hence, the *Bachelor*, filled to overflowing with barrels of profitable whale oil, responds to Ahab's question with the remark that it has only heard of Moby Dick but that it doesn't really believe in him. "Thou art too damned jolly," shouts Ahab. "Sail on!" Materialistic commercialism has neither the time nor the inclination for questions about the self. The *Rachel*, captained by an old friend of Ahab's, has ineffectually locked with Moby Dick the day before, but has lost a boat crew in doing so, including the captain's son. Ahab, however, is adamant in refusing to join the search and thus reveals some sort of drive with which neither humanity nor family can be allowed to interfere. The final gam is with the *Delight*, which has also recently met the white whale, been disastrously battered by it, and is now limping home in tatters, burying its dead on the way. The costly lesson it has well learned means nothing to Ahab. Subsidiary attitudes by Americans toward America are thus almost as varied *within* this novel as they are within the whole context of this essay.

The final, predestined confrontation is, of course, between Ahab and the whale. When Ahab, tangled in his own harpoon line, is dragged down, after the destruction of the *Pequod*, to his ocean-perishing, what rolls on in that "great shroud of the sea," rolling on "as it rolled five thousand years ago," is only the great white whale. The survival of Ishmael to tell the story, the disparity of motives between him and Ahab, the eclectic microcosmic representation of the mates and crew of the *Pequod*—all these and other refinements that contribute to the complex Americanism of this complex American novel must be passed over. But enough has been suggested here to make at least something for the case that Melville's account of the quest for the great white whale is in part also an account of the quest for an American identity. That his ultimate definition is somehow inscrutably involved with the interlocking destruction of Ahab and the survival of Ishmael is perhaps less important in this context than is his affirmation of the perpetuity of Moby Dick. Whatever the dramatized agonies of knowing what America is, Melville appears to me to be saying here, America as physical phenomenon and as idea inexorably, indestructibly exists—and will continue to exist as long as the great seas roll.

Milly Theale as America

The America in Henry James's *The Wings of the Dove* is something radically different, although there are affinities. Both Melville and James see their Americas as somehow going on forever. Both are crucially entranced imagistically with whiteness. But in most ways theirs are radically different novels, although I have on occasion asked students, with only a modicum of facetiousness, whether Milly Theale *is* Moby Dick.

James's novel is both an internationalized elegy and a nationalistic parable. The story is of the rich, beautiful, and dying Milly Theale, her move from America to London, and her meeting and developing involvement with Kate Croy and Merton Densher, two impecunious Britishers who are secretly engaged. Kate plots for Milly to fall in love with Densher, marry him, die, and leave him her vast wealth, then for her to marry Densher herself. The plot succeeds all too well—up to a point. Milly does fall in love with Densher, and although she discovers his liaison with Kate and does not marry him, she does die and leave him a fortune. The fortune, however, does not bring Kate and Densher together; in fact, it keeps them apart. But the central interest of the novel is not the relationship between Kate and Densher; it is instead the effect of Milly on them: the impact, to be succinct, of an American idea (as James conceives it) on a European compact.

James was always a great parable-maker, a sort of poetic mythologizer, but never perhaps more so than here, and he was perhaps nowhere (outside *The Ambassadors* and *The Golden Bowl*) so effective in portraying the international confrontations between his Americans and Europeans. It is exclusively to this parable, James's conception of its Americanness and his view of its ambivalent force and residue in Europe, that I wish to direct my attention.

On its most simplistic level, *The Wings of the Dove* can be viewed as an account of the proverbial American trickster (the confidence woman?): the country bumpkin (any American), set up for the take by the city slicker (any European), turns the tables by taking in the slicker himself. Milly, the intended victim of the nefarious plot, in fact becomes the victor; those who would have used her, Densher and Kate, end up neither with each other nor with Milly's fortune.

How James worked this out, what Kate and Densher got instead of one another or the fortune, what, in fact, Milly symbolically represents—make, of course, for James and for us, a great difference. At least part of what Milly is meant to represent James tells us directly in the preface to the novel: "To be the heir of all the ages," he says, "only to know yourself, as that consciousness should deepen, balked of your inheritance, would be to play the part, it struck me, or at least to arrive at the type, . . . on the whole the most becoming." In what sense she is *balked* is of course the crux of the matter. James is specifically referring to her health. But he might as well be referring also to her victimization. Is she, in fact, ultimately balked at all? She had loved and been loved in return. For Densher, we are told, "something had happened to him too beautiful and too sacred to describe. He had been . . . forgiven, dedicated, blessed." When, at the end of the novel, he discovers that Milly has left him her fortune in spite of the duplicity, when he makes Kate understand that he will marry her without the fortune but not with it, there develops a real Jamesian ambiguity about whether he rejects Kate or Kate rejects him.

There is, however, no ambiguity about what Densher becomes: a monkish ascetic worshiping at the shrine of the dead Milly, a shrine, Kate points out to him, that her death commanded. "She died," Kate tells him straight, without a flinch, "for you . . . that you might understand her." His memory of her, Kate tells him at the very end, is all he will need: "You're one for whom it will do. Her memory's your love. You *want* no other." "I'll marry you . . . in an hour," Densher responds. "As we were?" Kate asks. "As we were," he says. Kate's are the last words: "We shall never be again as we were!"

For James, Milly Theale is clearly an American idea— transmogrified, to be sure, into something half-Christ-like, something perhaps half-diabolical, exacting sweet revenge upon those who would have used her, all under the guise of a gesture of noble magnanimity, all with the result of having made of herself (at least for Densher) something endlessly to be adored, something endlessly to be worshiped.

For me the great scene of the novel, before the last one, has always been Milly's splendid dinner, the last time we see her directly in the novel. Milly, we are told, on this one occasion has been "let loose among them in a wonderful white dress." The effect on Densher, James continues, is that "she was different, younger, fairer, with the colour of her braided hair more than ever a not altogether lucky challenge to attention; yet he was loath wholly to explain it by her having quitted this once, for some obscure, yet doubtless charming reason, her almost monastic, her hitherto inveterate black." The whiteness of the dress, for Densher, transforms Milly into "the American girl as he had originally found her . . . in New York," into "the American girl . . . he had seen . . . in London." But he also sees the ambiguity; for, we are told, "he wouldn't have known whether to see in it [her white dress] an extension or a contraction of 'personality,' taking it as he did most directly for a confounding extension of surface." The magnificent power of Milly in white is even enough for once to shake Kate, who is here described as growing "a little pale" before her.

Kate nowhere underestimates Milly, is nowhere blind to the force and power she exerts as American, as wealth, as woman, and as idea. That her one blanch before Milly is in this magnificent scene and that Densher sees Milly's whiteness as a *"confounding* extension of surface" (emphasis added) all beautifully plays, of course, into my game, with its apparent ties to the whiteness of Melville's whale in *Moby-Dick*.

At the end, Kate is clear-sighted enough about what Densher has become. She sees, moreover, that he has come to love the idea more than he could ever have loved the fact. "Your change came," she says, "the day you last saw her; she died for you then."

But all the truth of Milly as America is a view that encompasses Kate's as completely as hers encompasses Densher's. James's total view, it goes without saying, radiates in a multiplicity of other directions that I have made no attempt here to indicate. Whatever else she is, however, Milly is here for James, in one central sense, *an* America. Whether divine or diabolical (or both), whatever she was or is, she lives on in the European Densher, after, indeed because of, her death. Her effect on others, James wrote in his preface to the novel, "would be as natural, these tragic, pathetic, ironic, these indeed for the most part sinister, liabilities, to her living associates, as they could be to herself as prime subject . . . and our young friend's existence would create . . . all round her, very much that whirlpool movement of the waters produced by the sinking of a big vessel . . . when we figure to ourselves the strong narrowing eddies, the immense force of suction, the general engulfment that, for any neighbouring object, makes immersion inevitable."

Thomas Sutpen as America

Sutpen's Hundred, Thomas Sutpen's barony in Yoknapatawpha County in Northern Mississippi, is as far removed from the salons and glitter of the rich in James's London and Venice as they themselves are from the rigors of whaling aboard the *Pequod* in Melville's wide Pacific. Yet, "the doomed baronial dream" of Sutpen encloses them both; for if Moby Dick can, in some sense, be seen as one America and Milly Theale, again in some sense, as another, then William Faulkner's *Absalom, Absalom!*, my thesis would seem to demand, must be seen here as something of both.

The rise and fall of Sutpen and his family recapitulates— perhaps prescribes—the American experience. It may, in addition, recapitulate the history of the world (from one perspective) and the history of the American South (from another). It may also recapitulate a Biblical parable (note the title), a Greek tragedy (note the action), a classic psychological and societal case (note the incest and miscegenation), and, most important, a history of literary forms (note the disparate points of view). The novel is unmistakably an experiment in literary technique. Sutpen never literally appears as a character at all; we get only several accounts of a phenomenon collectively *named* Thomas Sutpen.

The novel is the story of the four narrators (five, if we take into account the unmistakable voice of the unnamed narrator).[1] Their relations to, perspectives about, and accounts of this phenomenon called Sutpen are as varied as those of any other group of people would be who were of differing ages and sex and who had disparate backgrounds, experiences, and personalities. From these four narrators, and right at the center of the many other concepts that this complex novel presents, there emerges a picture of one American's life that in part is surely the life of all Americans. "Maybe it took . . . Thomas Sutpen to make all of us," we are told by Quentin.

Sutpen's history and Sutpen's Hundred are clear-cut paradigms of the American experience, although characteristic Faulknerian ones. The saga begins in 1807 with Sutpen's birth in West Virginia. It stops—but does not necessarily end—in 1909 with Sutpen's single survivor and sole inheritor, the black idiot Jim Bond, howling his outrage to the universe as the Sutpen mansion burns to the ground. The account of the rise and fall of Sutpen and his family, an account that must be extracted from the clearly biased, sometimes fabricated, and often contradictory accounts of the four narrators (a much-truncated chronology was provided by

Faulkner himself as an appendix to the novel), is just what makes of Sutpen and his history something roughly equivalent to a generic American and his history. Sutpen is born on a West Virginia mountaintop into a recently settled family of Anglo-Scottish stock. The rags-to-riches dream of a Paradise in the West is worked out in Sutpen's move from Haiti to Mississippi. The pragmatic marriage to the boss's daughter for the wherewithal to carry out the dream occurs in his early move to Haiti, where he makes his fortune through precisely such a marriage, although he renounces both that fortune (except for twenty black slaves) and his first-born son, Charles Bon, when he discovers his wife to be part black. The theme of a contradictory and ambivalent attitude toward the black is everywhere apparent: the renunciation in Haiti, the coupling twice with part or full blacks, the fear of miscegenation (for his daughter Judith) perhaps overriding his fear of incest when she falls in love with her part-black half-brother, Charles Bon. Thomas's son Henry murders his half-brother Charles for the same ambivalent reasons. Sutpen moves westward and acquires rich, fertile land (significantly from an Indian). The building of the paradise is on fecund bottom land. It is destroyed in the holocaust of the Civil War. The downfall of the family is the result of a grand design, a dream, imperfectly understood and much too rigidly conceived. Finally, the inheritance is an inheritance not only of whatever the America is that Thomas Sutpen symbolically represents but of the whole world.

In the marvelous last page of the novel this prophetic interchange occurs between Shreve McCannon, the Canadian-born student, and Quentin Compson.

> "So it took Charles Bon and his mother to get rid of old Tom, and Charles Bon and the octoroon to get rid of Judith, and Charles Bon and Clytie to get rid of Henry; and Charles Bon's mother and Charles Bon's grandmother got rid of Charles Bon. So it takes two niggers to get rid of one Sutpen, don't it . . . ? Which is all right, it's fine; it clears the whole ledger, you can tear all the pages out and burn them, except for one thing. And do you know what that is? . . . You've got one nigger left. One nigger Sutpen left. Of course you can't catch him and you don't even always see him and you never will be able

to use him. But you've got him there still. You still hear him at night sometimes. Don't you?"

"Yes," Quentin said.

"And so you know what I think . . . ?"

"No," Quentin said.

"Then I'll tell you. I think that in time the Jim Bonds are going to conquer the western hemisphere. Of course it won't quite be in our time and of course as they spread toward the poles they will bleach out again like the rabbits and the birds do, so they won't show up so sharp against the snow. But it will still be Jim Bond; and so in a few thousand years, I who regard you will also have sprung from the loins of African kings."

Great books, Wright Morris once wrote (referring to Henry James's *The American Scene*), not only tell the truth about the now and the then. They prophesy; they prescribe the future. *Absalom, Absalom!* was published in 1936. Whatever else it is, it has been cannily prophetic, prescribing in one way not only what America *was* and *is* but what it appears to be *becoming* during very recent years.

In the context here, of course, the curious connection, the clinching tie, is the white snow Shreve envisions and its symbolic links with the whiteness of Melville's whale and of Milly Theale's dress. "The Jim Bonds," Shreve says, "are going to conquer the western hemisphere. . . . They will bleach out like the rabbits and the birds do, so they won't show up so sharp against the snow." But his last phrase is not necessarily a pessimistic one: for "I who regard you will have sprung from the loins of African kings."

Moreover, the last word is Quentin's, not Shreve's. To Shreve's final, facetious, ironic, all-comic, all-tragic "Now I want you to tell me just one thing more. Why do you hate the South?" Quentin responds, "*I dont hate it . . . I dont. I dont! I dont hate it!*" Neither, I suspect, do we—in all the rich, complex, symbolic senses that marvelous *it* encompasses.

Modern America Foreseen?

As the title I have given to this exegesis states, I am here discussing only three Americas. The many other Americas that could be mentioned in this context are as varied as the writers capable of conceiving them. But because these three Americas are the Americas of (in my opinion) our three best novelists, Americas from among, moreover, the best novels of these three novelists, this aspect of their varied symbolic visions should have a special worth. For, unalike and uncommon as they are, the Americas they have projected do have some things in common: cosmic scope, prophecy, a strange, complex, wholly American double vision about the ambivalent nature of whiteness, and perpetuity. Ishmael is bubbled-up from the sunken *Pequod* to tell the story of the great white whale that will last as long as the great seas roll; Milly Theale will live forever in the mind of Merton Densher, who is now forgiven, dedicated, blessed; and the bleached Jim Bonds who will inherit this earth will have sprung from the loins of African kings.

I stated in the final comment of my introductory remarks to this essay that in at least one special sense recent books of Bellow, Malamud, and Updike were "old" novels. Conversely, I hope to have shown that the three old novels here discussed at such length may in turn be seen, again in at least one special sense, as very "new" ones. For in this context the three symbolic Americas they conceive become very recent Americas indeed: a land that destroys those who would madly destroy it, an ideal of selflessness that may well also be self-serving, and a tragic heritage that becomes prophetically humane. Problems of American ecology, American self-righteousness, and American racism were never more with us than now.

THREE

Benjy Compson, Jake Barnes, and Nick Carraway

Replication in Three "Innocent" American Narrators of the 1920s

THE MOST ORIGINAL, audacious, and self-conscious concept of innocence in American fiction during the 1920s appeared near the end of the decade in the first section of the second Yoknapatawpha novel of William Faulkner, that is, in the Benjy section of *The Sound and the Fury*, published in 1929. That novel began, Faulkner later reported many times, "as a short story . . . a story without plot, of some children being sent away from the house during the[ir] grandmother's funeral. They were too young to be told what was going on and they saw things only incidentally to the childish games they were playing . . . the lugubrious matter of removing the corpse from the house, etc. . . ." In what Michael Millgate describes as the novelist's "fullest account of how *The Sound and the Fury* came to be written," Faulkner later stated:

> The idea struck me to see how much more I could have got out of the idea of the blind, self-centeredness of innocence, typified by children, if one of those children had been truly innocent, that is, an idiot. So the idiot was born and then I became interested in the relationship of the idiot to the world that he was in but would never be able to cope with and just where could he get the tenderness, the help, to shield him in his innocence. I mean "innocence" in the sense that God had stricken him blind at birth, that is, mindless at birth, there was nothing he could ever do about it.[1]

In concept at least, therefore, innocence is right at the self-conscious center of whatever Faulkner first conceived his dearest and for many his most respected novel to be. What it in fact *came* to be in the finished novel will be examined later in the context of two additional innocent narrators of the 1920s.

Three years earlier, in 1926, Ernest Hemingway had first gained fame with *The Sun Also Rises*, a novel that was almost immediately acclaimed the masterpiece it has for the most part continuously been judged since. Perhaps not so much in concept as in execution, it may well represent the idealized other side of innocence, that is, an *un*conscious representation of innocence at once on a par with and yet distinctly different from what we now understand Faulkner's conception of Benjy to have been.

The third major writer I want to consider here, F. Scott

Fitzgerald, precedes both Faulkner and Hemingway. The text is *The Great Gatsby*, published in 1925 and long since recognized as among the most exalted and ceremonial studies of American innocence. Jay Gatsby himself is the figure most often pointed to as the great commemorative example of that innocence, as perhaps he should be. Thus, some attention to him here is inevitable. My more central interest is Nick Carraway, a more provocative embodier of innocence. As narrator, moreover, he relates directly to Jake Barnes and to Benjy and helps better to bring into focus the central concern of this exercise: the portrayed innocent narrator as a replica of a central aesthetic concern of some American novelists of the 1920s.

Faulkner, Hemingway, and Fitzgerald constitute the peaks of American fiction of that decade. Even so, the special, limited context of this essay should not blind one to the rich and varied larger contexts of which it is a part: the context of the other work by each of these novelists no less than that of twentieth-century American writers in general; the cultural, social, political, and literary context of the 1920s no less than the more particularized context of American fiction of the same period.[2]

Another aside about another larger context is perhaps also appropriate here: the use of the word *innocent*. Its use here can only be suggestive, not precise, for the precision must eventually come from the specialized context of this clearly specialized subject. Still, innocent is the word I would use to describe Hester Prynne at the end of *The Scarlet Letter* when she implores Arthur Dimmesdale to assure her of some happy life everlasting as recompense for all their woe. It is a term also applicable to many of Melville's protagonists, from Tommo of *Typee* (in his foolish search for the happy vale) to that complex of explicit confrontations that makes up half of the ultimate dramatic conflict between Billy Budd and the forces arrayed against him in Melville's last tale. Henry James's view of Emerson's "ripe unconsciousness of evil," his "little sense for the dark, the foul, the base,"[3] is a reference to still another manifestation of innocence. Although it was Mark Twain, not Henry James, who titled his first book *The Innocents Abroad*, James shows us more frequent, pervasive, various, and complex conceptions of that term. However, neither these subjective applications of the term to nineteenth-century American writing nor those more formalized ones in such intellectual histories as R. W. B. Lewis's *The American Adam* or Leo Marx's *The Machine in the Garden* are as important here as simply what we see the uses of innocence to be in the three works. They define their own terms; they create their own special context.

The Example of Faulkner

Benjy, of course, is not the only innocent among the Compsons. He is, however, the primal, innermost core, the center pole, as it were, around which the more sophisticated concepts of his brothers Quentin and Jason are wrapped and shaped. Although one of the great conceptual achievements of *The Sound and the Fury* is the brilliant variety of rubrics by which this triad of brothers can be viewed (as stages of history, as kinds of poetry, as theories of time, as ages of man, and as psychological components, among many others), central to all, however varied and different the levels, is their mutual inadequacy to the simple challenge of their sister Caddy's at least comparatively normal growth. Nothing defines more precisely both their values and their limitations than their relations and reactions to her. To be sure, they also define what she is. But she in turn defines them. The modes, methods, and means through which these reciprocal definitions occur are ultimately as important as the definitions themselves.

Benjy, the last of the sons, by inversion is paradoxically the beginning. If his perspective first appears to be the most extreme of the three, it finally reveals itself to be instead the most direct, the most pure. Born an idiot, "mindless at birth," Faulkner says, Benjy is one of "the truly innocent." Insofar as they exist at all, his rational faculties are rendered simply as a series of cameralike impressions that happen to him on the single day of 7 April 1928. But those impressions, we soon discover, are of events not only of that single day but also of the past as linked by simple imagistic, tactile, auditory, or olfactory associations. Thus, for Benjy (because he has no sense of time) and at first for us (because his method of perception is one the reader has to learn) the past is rendered *literally* and on the most direct level as indistinguishable from the present. This primal concept of innocence, the inability to distinguish past from present (and brilliantly rendered directly to us through events as Benjy narrates them), has its other thematic ramifications. Change, for example, becomes unthinkable; change is precisely the mode in Caddy that Benjy cannot tolerate.

The embryonic image of the book, Faulkner also stated, is that of "the picture of the little girl's muddy drawers, climbing that tree to look in the parlor window with her brothers that didn't have the courage to climb the tree[,] waiting to see what she saw."[4] Those stained drawers become emblematic of the "sin" of her affairs, leading eventually to her illegitimate daughter Quentin and its ramifications (especially for her brothers Quentin and Jason), just as they are emblematic of her "fortunate fall" into the primeval slime, in contrast to those waiting brothers who, Faulkner said, "didn't have the courage to climb the tree." But that tree is suggestive of still another element (aside from its beautiful structural rightness as that down which, at the end of the Benjy section, the girl Quentin is described as descending).[5] For it is only when Caddy has about her the smell of trees—while still childlike, that is—that she is acceptable to Benjy.

That other object that he loves so dearly, the golf course that had been made from a pasture and sold to provide money to send Quentin to Harvard, is ultimately symbolic of that same natural innocence suggested by the smell of trees, especially when one ponders the implications of Faulkner's inspired choices for their defining contrastive opposites, the unnatural perfume that growing Caddy uses that sends Benjy howling and the fruitless, manicured, and meaningless golf course. The tie of tree to pasture is obvious enough in light of these modern foils. That tree, incidentally, is given still another symbolic twist (in Faulkner's "fifth" version of the novel, the appendix, and in his interview with Jean Stein) when he specifies the tree that the girl with the muddy drawers climbs as a *pear* tree and that which the girl Quentin climbs down as a *rain pipe*. The contrast of pear tree to rain pipe is clear enough, especially in the context of the smell of trees to the smell of perfume and of pasture to golf course.[6] The third object of Benjy's love, the firelight, is directly equated by Faulkner with what he calls "the same shape of sleep" (*SAF*, p. 19), a brightly glowing nothingness; for sleep, however variously symbolic, can also be seen as the opposite of overt awareness, action, cognition, movement.

Benjy Compson is thus the innocent par excellence. Frederick J. Hoffman is surely right in describing "his as the moral order of an age of innocence, . . . an order that is rigidly upheld in his every response."[7] Accruing levels of innocence are also embodied in Faulkner's conceptions of Quentin and Jason, both of which are centrally defined, as was his conception of Benjy, by attitudes toward and reactions to the rise and fall of Caddy; only brief attention can be given to those conceptions here, however, for the chief concern is still with Benjy.

Suffice it to point out, therefore (as has been pointed out many times), that Quentin's inadequacies are basically the same as Benjy's.[8] Only his means and concepts, his methods and modes, his *tone*, appear so strikingly different. Both brothers want to fix Caddy's life into the stasis of childhood. Both confront dislocations between past and present. Both manifest ineluctable despair at Caddy's movement through time in contrast to their embrace of time held still. Both inevitably fail. In contrast to Benjy's simple, sensory, almost photographic moments are Quentin's obsessive formulations, ratiocinations, conceptualizations. Benjy is indifferent to time; Quentin is obsessed with it. For Benjy the past is the present; for Quentin the present is the past. A moment of remembered order suffices to quiet Benjy. Quentin's parallel quiet requires an intricately conceptualized, ordered rationale for suicide. The ultimate effect is therefore one of complement, not of contrast; one of parallel, not of opposition. Benjy and Quentin are both innocents.

So, in his quite different way, is Jason. He too fails to cope with Caddy, and he fails, moreover, as do the other two, within the terms he lives by as clearly as their failures are confined within theirs. Caddy's "sin," for him, is "breach of contract"—to wit, the promised bank job that is not finally forthcoming because of Caddy's annulled marriage to Herbert Head. His defeat in the end by the fruit of that original sin, Miss Quentin, is indeed, as one critic has nicely called it, a marvelous kind of "legal illegal irony, for in stealing his money Miss Quentin is not only getting her own back but also acting in the manner and spirit of Jason himself."[9] Much more deserves to be said about Jason, but perhaps enough has been said simply to establish him as the innocent mercantilist among those other Compson innocents, Benjy and his brother Quentin.

Leaving these two complements to Benjy, we can return to him through another perspective. Numerous critics have drawn numerous possible sources and literary parallels to Quentin and Jason.[10] But the Benjy section is another story. Cleanth Brooks, to be sure, has seen in it a "kind of primitive poetry, a poetry of the senses, rendered with great immediacy."[11] But the more typical response is that of Millgate, who sees it "as more exclusively Faulkner's invention" than the other two,[12] or perhaps this more extended estimation by Joseph Reed: "Our response to Benjy must be new with this book—we have seen something like it (but not at all exactly like it) in any attempt at stream-of-consciousness. We are familiar in poetry with the dreamlike qualities of pure perception divorced from cognition and intellection, but the response called up by Benjy is not parallel to any conventional or familiar fictional response."[13]

Reed has his own elaborate formulation of what that response should be. It deserves expression in his own words. After first observing that "Benjy comes first not just because he casts the reader adrift but because he gives him a place to stand" and that "his narrative is more significant as clarification than as obfuscation," he makes this extended point:

> Benjy's first-person narrative takes us out of our normal sympathies and fictional empathies, preoccupations upon which the effect of a first-person narrative normally depends, which it cultivates, by which it seduces. It subjects us to an entirely new mode of perception. It is not because it is a tale told by an idiot that we are jolted, it is that the idiot's tale so perfectly orders the perceptions, associations, and thematic relationships, makes them so inescapable, that we forget our normal stock sympathies and participations in the fictional world and move in a different step. We do not "become" Benjy because that would betray the peculiarity of his position, the subtlety of the free association which connect sections, so clearly his and his alone. We don't

identify closely enough with him and his patterns to
become anything like him. The section is less a realistic
rendering of the author's adoption of Benjy's consciousness than it is an exercise in the control of limited
language to a poetic end. The construction is as "literary" as chapter 33 of James's *Golden Bowl*, yet it spins
itself out with the ease of the babble of Benjy's mind. The
different step in which we move is timed to a literary or
poetic end rather than to that of a precise representation
of consciousness.[14]

This is a suggestive formulation in any number of ways. I
want to explore only one of them, connecting Faulkner's concept of innocence in the Benjy section with the reminder that
Benjy's mind is in fact also a narrator's mind, or at least a surrogate for one, and is consequently the surrogate for a special
kind of tale telling, a special kind of artist. For that which
defines what he is has simultaneously to define, through the
kind of events and the order of events he is depicted as rendering, the special kind of narrator *and* of narrating he represents.

Therefore, one must of course agree with Reed that it is to
"a literary or poetic end" that we are forced to step. But
precisely what that end is must also be dependent, at least in
part, on what the narrator himself is rendered as being.
James's dictum that action is character holds as well here as
in other contexts. Hence, the two-leveled action of Benjy is,
on the one hand, sparse and highly selective, *contractive*, but
still symbolic enough in its beginnings and end, the movements from the edge of the golf course in the company of
Luster to the witnessed flight of Quentin, with emphasized
moments of loss (the golf course) and of pain (the fire) in
between. The remembered action, on the other hand, is much
richer, more immediately far-reaching, *expansive*, touching
many events between the day of Damuddy's death in 1898
and the shapeless sleep at the end of Benjy's day, and many
of them also marked by loss or pain: Caddy's use of perfume,
Caddy in the swing with Charlie, Caddy's loss of virginity,
Caddy's wedding, Benjy's assault on the Burgess girl and his
castration, the successive deaths of Damuddy, Quentin, and
Mr. Compson. The details of this two-leveled action have
long since been worked out in any number of handbooks and

Faulkner guides.[15] But the point of how this contractive-expansive effect is achieved can be put more directly.

That which distances the reader at the same time that it intricately involves him can perhaps be illustrated with the single example of the caddie-Caddy connection in the opening pages. In the first place, the abrupt conjunction itself is of a kind and through a mode that is much too estranged from our normal perceptual processes to allow us to become Benjy. It thus *distances* us, for the conjunction is made simply as a kind of enjambment of given event to given event, one crawl through a fence against another. Benjy's lacks intensify this distancing—his lack of cognition, of the power to verbalize, of a sense of time, of an apparent ability to distinguish between good and evil—all precisely elements the reader himself must begin to provide. Hence, the involvement. Eventually, of course, in and through that ultimate in intricate involvement, the caddie-Caddy event becomes intelligible, the degree of intelligibility becomes in a way the degree of the involvement. Thus the prod, the simple similarity of sounds, forces us to provide the words (we know the difference between a golf caddie and a girl named Caddy). We provide a concept of time (we know the difference between past and present). We probably even supply a judgment (we at least like to think we can make distinctions between good and evil). But a moral judgment at this point is also very close to an aesthetic judgment—it so clearly involves process—that we spiral back out, distancing. Only at some far distant remove do we remember finally that we are also to know that an inarticulate whimpering moan at the sight of a golf caddie disappearing over a hill—in all of those both involved and distanced perspectives that we now have—is precisely the appropriate poetic response (because now so comprehensive a response) that it in fact is.

It was a brave and ingenious concept of innocence and of narration, and when its corollaries, both within the novel and without, begin to come into focus, we may see with a new perspective how a look backward may sometimes become also a look forward. Within the novel, for example, Benjy becomes the norm by which we judge others. Their indifference, their love, their cruelty emerge as almost precise responses to his mindless state, the reader's responses to them following fast upon their responses to him. What better signals Dilsey's

value than her treatment of Benjy? When the symbolic configurations within the Benjy section itself—both the present
action and the past action, both as things in themselves and
as an interconnected whole—are expanded to become the
symbolic configurations of the novel as a whole, the centrality
of Benjy's condition as innocent and as narrator becomes apparent. Perhaps more than enough has already been said
about the accruing concepts of innocence as represented by
Quentin and Jason. Certainly, less than enough has been
said about Benjy's role in the important last section of the
novel. But the subject here is Benjy as narrator. *His* moan as
provoked by the Caddy/Quentin "fall" is in some central
sense comprehensive enough.

The Example of Hemingway

To view Hemingway's Jake Barnes as an innocent is not a
novel observation. His profession, in some ways, almost prescribes that condition. A reporter, an observer, is, almost by
definition, precluded from being a participator, a doer. When
this profession of the novel's narrator is joined to his condition as a man, his literal and symbolic phallic wound from
the war, Jake Barnes becomes a kind of necessary innocent
as a "given" of the novel's opening situation. This conception,
therefore, would seem likely to prescribe something central
in the novel's overall strategy. Jake's larger symbolic roles as
reflector of the condition of post–World War I man, his "Fisher
King" mask, his *Waste Land* ties and residuals, his Hugh
Selwyn Mauberly–like ramifications—in short, his various
Lost Generationisms—are all in no way inconsistent with
this more basic role as enforced observer, as interpreter, and,
through that observation and interpretation, as subject himself. As it does any dramatized narrator, what Jake tells us
about others becomes a way of defining what he is.

The triangulated experiential subject at the center of Jake's
observation would seem, in its very simplest form, to run
something like this: Because impotent narrator is hopelessly
in love with beautiful heroine (and she with him), beautiful
heroine, Lady Brett Ashley, becomes, in her frustration, pro-

miscuous woman engaged to impotent narrator's best friend. Promiscuous woman, while still engaged, takes on, then rejects, two "outside" lovers—Robert Cohn and Pedro Romero, Romantic Hero and Code Hero, respectively, to use the terms Mark Spilka has long since given them.[16] She eventually banishes Romantic Hero to save herself from *his* romantic tone. She later banishes Code Hero to save *him* from *her* corruption. Finally, she returns to impotent narrator to dream about what might have been between them. Impotent narrator responds ambiguously to what they both now are.

Such an account does more than a little disservice to many aspects of the novel: its magnificent sense of place (Paris, Burguete, Pamplona, San Sebastian, Madrid), its style, its tone. It is nevertheless an accurate account and perhaps thereby suggestive enough of how perilously thin its basic substance is. For it appears to be, in fact, a peculiar strategy of this novel that this triptych of characters—Cohn, Romero, and Brett—serve as the best key to Jake. He identifies with each in turn, sometimes consciously, sometimes, apparently, not. He is as locked to both men, at least intermittently, as they are successively locked to Brett. At times, moreover, he acquiesces with such completeness to everything that Brett is that he appears to be literally at one with her. What, if anything, is left over outside of what he is *as them* remains to be seen.

Jake as Romero almost every reader of the novel would accept. When Jake explains to Brett how "Romero's bullfighting gave real emotion, because he kept the absolute purity of line in his movements and always quietly and calmly let the horns pass him close each time," he follows it by saying that "Romero had the old thing, the holding of his purity of line through the maximum of exposure."[17] Who doubts that this is not what, in good moments, Jake saw himself as being? Romero's taking a brutal beating from the enraged Cohn without a whimper, "not knowing how to box, yet never staying down" (as Richard Hovey has put it[18]), is obviously idealized conduct in Jake's eyes. When Brett dismisses the bullfighter in Madrid because, she says, "I'm not going to be one of these bitches that ruins children" (*SAR*, p. 243), Romero departs without a whimper, paying his own bill. Clearly, for Jake, that is the way such exits should be made.

We, as distinguished from Jake, see Romero as a courageous, handsome, unspoiled youth, a *budding* matador. Brett repeatedly calls him a child (*SAR*, p. 167, for example). Even the aficionado Montoya refers to him as a "boy" (*SAR*, p. 172). At least two critics make much of how the conduct of an ideal young matador is quite far removed from that of Romero.[19] Consequently, his vulnerability to Brett, like his invulnerability to Cohn's pounding, reveals a streak of youthful romanticism in Romero as deep as that in Cohn, albeit from a different culture and hence a different kind. But whatever the kind, Jake Barnes as a youthful Romero is a very "innocent" Jake Barnes indeed, given *his* condition and experience.

Jake as Robert Cohn is somewhat more complicated—although the identification is, if anything, even more unmistakably established than it is with Romero. Cohn's youthful romanticism is a more explicit "given" of the novel. At the same time, Jake "becomes" Cohn in a much more intricate and indirect way. One of the curious inversions in this novel is that Cohn's steadfast devotion to an ideal of love appears to be held in such low repute. To be sure, his Jewishness is an issue, as are his dislike of alcohol, his refusal to leave when he is told to do so, and his fatal outsider's "tone." He has, moreover, the audacity to view the bullfight from the point of view of the bull—"It's no life being a steer" (*SAR*, p. 141)— and he finds the goring of the horse sickening. But there is no reason to think that Cohn would not, or has not, "paid the bill" as fully as Romero has or that, were the roles reversed in the famous fist fight, Cohn would not take physical defeat in the same style that Romero does. Jake himself tells us that he was a good loser, that he was "not angry at being beaten." In fact, "he was very nice about it" (*SAR*, p. 45). No, as Arthur Scott pointed out years ago, Romero and Cohn have "more in common with each other than with any other of the characters." They are both "outsiders" to this group. "They both love not wisely but too well, but at least they do love,"[20] as in his way Jake does. And, of course, they are both children.

Jake's explicit identification with Cohn has been fully worked out by Spilka.[21] Significantly, it results from Jake's own most adolescent action in the book—his turning the boy Romero over to Brett out of some boyish impulse of his own to acquiesce in Brett's every whim. That it is indeed a boyish impulse is strongly supported by Jake's dredging up (for the only time in the book) a memory of his youthful football days following his knockout blow from Cohn upon Cohn's wrathful discovery of the now-joined Brett and Romero. Jake's vivid memory of how he felt as a boy coming home after a crack on the head during an out-of-town football game is sustained right up to his visit to Cohn's room, to which he has returned following his fight with Romero and where Jake finds him "face down on the bed crying. He had on a white polo shirt, the kind he'd worn at Princeton" (*SAR*, pp. 193–94). Jake's identification with Cohn at this point is complete. Spilka is surely right in the part of his conclusion that applies to this point: "The truth about Barnes seems obvious now: he has always been an emotional adolescent."[22]

Jake's third identification, that with Brett, is significantly enough made at this same point. Having made it, it perhaps becomes also the point at which his adolescent skin begins to be washed away. The symbolic tie is indeed with *bathing*, the restorative word that Brett uses repeatedly. Her "I must get a bath" is characteristic enough (*SAR*, pp. 144, 159). But here it becomes Jake's totem. Reminded that Cohn called him a pimp, Jake responds: "I did not care. I wanted a hot bath. I wanted a hot bath in deep water." He repeats the phrase a few lines later. "I'm going to take a bath" (*SAR*, p. 194). This is more than enough preparation for his more deeply symbolic bathing (and thus cleansing) in the deep green waters at San Sebastian, to which he flies after the departure of Cohn alone and of Brett with Romero. Jake's total acceptance of Brett's values up to this point, moreover, has seemingly never been questioned—even up to and including her lust for Romero. We see him in tears when he is alone in bed at night, but her actions up to this point—her engagement to Mike, her affairs with Cohn and with Romero—are for him not to be questioned. His apparent rationale is their "impossible" love given his "unreasonable wound."

Jake's final return to Brett after her final dismissal of Romero drives home all the more clearly what their relationship in truth has been. Jake is apparently on the edge of seeing it himself in his description of his own action at Brett's call for him to return: "That was it. Send a girl off with one man. Introduce her to another to go off with him. Now go and bring her back. And sign the wire with love" (*SAR*, p. 239). Brett's last line makes it equally clear that she has seen nothing: "Oh, Jake . . . we could have had such a damned good time together." Jake's famous retort, "Yes . . . Isn't it pretty to think so," at least leaves his options open.

Jake *acts* very little in this novel. What he *observes* is almost everything. He observes, moreover, with such persuasive, even celebrated vividness that it is easy to lose sight of how very little Jake himself does. Hovey's observation that "Jake is so passive . . . that through the course of the narrative he does only three things: (1) expresses his love for Brett, mostly verbally, and serves as her confidant; (2) pimps for her; and (3) goes to Madrid when she asks him to rescue her"[23] may be an exaggeration, but not by much. What he observes and how he observes, however, are something else. The "what," to some extent, has already been indicated. The "how" is equally important.

At base, Jake is simply a recorder of the world around him. His own reflections about what events mean are so minimized as to be almost nonexistent. Indeed, that he observes so much and "sees" so little is precisely the concept that makes his "innocence" so functional. Like Faulkner's method, the method here demands that the reader formulate meaning— out of what and how Jake does record and then, through that, out of the character himself. Jake, for example, appears to make nothing of his early association with Georgette the prostitute and then of their joining with Brett and the homosexuals. That meeting is comment itself of a sort in its abrupt transition to Jake and Brett alone for the first time. It is immediately apparent to the reader that Count Mippipopolous is meant as foil and thus measurer of a kind to Jake, but this is not at all apparent to Jake. The celebrated fishing interlude to Burguete does reveal some self-conscious irony and thus meaning in the well-known "irony and pity" parody but apparently none at all in its placement as preface to the idyllic fishing scene itself. Whereas the reader is probably meant to see the simple orderliness of the Burguete episode as a preparatory contrast or restorative relief to the *dis*ordered rage on the plains below at Pamplona or at Paris, it is the simple orderliness of, say, fish to fern that for Jake seems to mean as much as anything else: "I took the trout ashore, washed them in the cold, smoothly heavy water above the dam, and then picked some ferns and packed them all in the bag, three trout on a layer of ferns, then another layer of ferns, then three more trout, and then covered them with ferns. They looked nice in the ferns" (*SAR*, pp. 119–20).

Fish to fern as a kind of simple ordering principle may in fact mark as well as any Hemingway's subtle and original way of having Jake's relatively unconscious placements carry so much more meaning for us than they can have for him. Prostitute to homosexual, Jake to Count, Burguete to Pamplona, and, most importantly, Cohn to Romero (and Jake to Brett)—all force us to create for ourselves meaning beyond that of which Jake himself appears capable. Only when he is told to his face, and in the simple direct language that even a child could understand, that his true relation to Brett is as pimp to whore, does he begin to see what he has been and what he is.

Jake's innocence is that of an adolescent, not that of a mindless Benjy, but it is a kind of innocence, nevertheless. Moreover, it is inextricably entwined with Jake's role as narrator, as observer and as teller. His condition *is* his method; they define each other. In the absence of any specific comments by Hemingway (of the kind we have from Faulkner) about what he originally conceived Jake to be, we are forced to rely wholly on the text. But knowing what we do know about Hemingway generally, about Jake's relation to the earlier Nick Adams and to the later Frederic Henry, and about the more than superficial relations of all of those characters to what we perhaps too often like to think Hemingway considered himself to be, it is doubtful that Hemingway would have described Jake Barnes as any kind of innocent. On the other hand, Hemingway is so much the dedicated artist, so true and pure, in his best moments, in his devotion to the principle of rendering his material honestly as he perceives it that the stylistic honesty itself corrects the apparent intention and thus results in a special kind of aesthetic authenticity that ultimately is its own best definition. The clean purity of a state of innocence, therefore, can be an aesthetic plus whatever the ethical level of the subject it is rendering.

The Example of Fitzgerald

The most complicated of the three examples of the innocent narrator to be considered here is that in *The Great Gatsby*. For in that volume we have a narrator who, if anything, is all too avowedly self-conscious in *his* rendering of a concept of innocence, the virtues and vices of the ceremonial Jay Gatsby. Gallons of ink have been given over to the ramifications of that concept. Far less has been given to the perhaps more central issue, how Nick Carraway's concept of Gatsby is itself a more deeply rimmed reflection of himself.[24] The tactic is quite simple and direct: Daisy is to Gatsby as Gatsby is to Nick. The meaning, however, becomes expansively complex.

Nick is by far the most sophisticated of our narrators, and the glittering felicities of his style make his case for Gatsby a very attractive and persuasive one indeed. But when baldly expressed and given chronologically, the "real" history of Gatsby is depressing enough. Born James Gatz of nondescript and unsuccessful farmers somewhere in the Midwest, a young ambitious boy of seventeen becomes through eager happenstance the confidant and factotum to one Dan Cody, a rapacious old millionaire who spends most of his time on his private yacht. Jay Gatsby (he changes his name when he first joins Cody) serves in this capacity for five years, traveling widely and learning the advantages of not drinking, of the power of his smile, and of how to ignore women. He sees, moreover, the power of money in action. Cody dies in 1917 and leaves Gatsby a legacy of twenty-five thousand dollars, which Gatsby, however, never receives.

At this point Gatsby enters the army, and by another "colossal accident" meets Daisy Fay, a beautiful girl of the upper classes, whom Gatsby considers to be the only "nice" girl he has ever known. They fall in love and have a brief affair, but Gatsby has to sail for Europe. While he is away, Daisy marries the enormously rich Tom Buchanan of Chicago. They have one daughter and eventually settle in East Egg, on Long Island. The widely decorated Gatsby, now a major but penniless from the war, makes a sentimental trip to Louisville while Daisy is on her honeymoon and correctly guesses, as Hoffman so neatly puts it, that "it was not Tom but the money that had finally convinced her. To win her back, he would have to 'buy her,' to exceed in ostentation and power the wealth of Buchanan's inheritance."[25]

How Gatsby *acquires* his great wealth is very sketchily given. All we know for a fact—and that by the word of the gangster Wolfsheim, "the man who fixed the World Series back in 1919"[26]—is that he is found and sponsored by the racketeer, that he still works for or with him and consequently is inevitably involved with various illegalities of the prohibition era, and that he is enormously successful. When the book opens, he has quietly and tenaciously maneuvered himself into a colossal mansion in West Egg, across the bay from the Buchanans, to be as close as he can to Daisy.

The action of the book from this point can be put even more succinctly. Through the help of Nick Carraway, his neighbor and Daisy's cousin, and through his wealth he reenters Daisy's life and eventually puts forth his prior claim to her. He is of course rejected. But before Gatsby quite surely knows this, he is killed by the husband of Tom Buchanan's mistress, Myrtle Wilson, who was accidentally run down by Daisy when she was driving Gatsby's car. Gatsby has of course assumed the blame, and Tom Buchanan, also of course, has covertly identified him for Wilson. The Buchanans move away, and Nick makes arrangements for Gatsby's funeral and buries him.

It is this simple, sordid story that Nick relates several months later. But what a difference in the way he tells it! And what still another difference when we begin to realize that *how* Nick tells us the history of Gatsby indicates more centrally his own history.

Like Gatsby, Nick is also a native of the Midwest. Also like Gatsby, he is a veteran of World War I. His school, however, is Yale, an ironic parallel to Gatsby's two weeks in a small Lutheran college in southern Minnesota. He also settles in the East (to pursue his career as a bond salesman for the Probity Trust in New York City), though his lodging is a small rented house in West Egg, next door to Gatsby's magnificent mansion. He too has had girls in his vague, mysterious past, and he is also to court, at least for a time, a corrupt woman, the socialite cheating golfer Jordan Baker. But what he comes to court more assiduously is the meaning of Gatsby, and what he finally asserts that meaning to be is nothing less than the American Dream itself, as he reformulates for us, back now in the Midwest, the events of that tawdry summer.

Fitzgerald gives us a Nick who is a wit and a moralist, possessed, moreover, with a mythologizing, parable-making imagination and an accompanying way with words as glitteringly captivating as perhaps any character in American literature. His compulsion to expand the events of that summer into *the* American experience is consequently so persuasive that it is only in retrospect that we begin to see that expansion as possibly a self-serving description of himself.

Who can resist the feigned distancing of Nick's celebrated preamble to Gatsby's curiously singular appeal, this "man who represented everything for which I have an unaffected scorn" because "there was something gorgeous about him, some heightened sensitivity to the promises of life," some "extraordinary gift for hope, a romantic readiness such as I have never found in any other person and which it is not likely I shall ever find again" (*GG*, p. 2)? When it is precisely "that flabby impressionability which is dignified under the name of the 'creative temperament'" that is specified as what Gatsby is not, who, at first reading, is to object? When he concludes that famous opening with the judgment that "Gatsby turned out all right at the end; it is what preyed on Gatsby, what foul dust floated in the wake of his dreams" that was the problem (*GG*, p. 2), we believe him.

The parallels between the extensions of Gatsby's meanings and the successive uncoverings of his past are no less compelling—even when they are given as if the more prosaic the fact, the more grandiose the meaning. This is nowhere more clear than at the end of the novel when we get our first account of Gatsby's earliest years. There the appearance of his nondescript father and the sordid, squalid funeral are sad contrasts to Nick's equation of Gatsby's dream with the "fresh, green breast of the new world" (*GG*, p. 182). Such comparisons occur throughout the novel and for a variety of purposes: the green light on the end of Daisy's dock to the "silver pepper of the stars" that Gatsby observes (*GG*, p. 21); Wolfsheim's cufflinks of human molars (*GG*, p. 73) to Daisy's pearls. Of course, it is the valley of ashes that is the truly celebrated example of this kind of equation in *The Great Gatsby*. There, a bountiful and peaceful plenitude metaphorically "controls" the crumbling, powdery, desolate valley of ashes that the valley in fact is. That "wild wag of an oculist" to whom is attributed the inspiration of Dr. T. J. Eckleburg's eyes—"blue and gigantic—their retinas are one yard high" (*GG*, p. 23)— is also in fact that one wild wag of a narrator, Nick. Who indeed can resist him?

Perhaps only Fitzgerald himself.

Clearly built into the very core and conception of the novel are the parallel appeals of Daisy for Gatsby and of Gatsby for Nick—the alluring appeal of the very rich, the irrelevance of the corrupting fact when posed against the abstracting ideal, the adolescent dream as exclusive rubric to the condition of now. Nick's imagination feeds on Gatsby's wealth no less ravenously than Gatsby's does on Daisy's—his colossal mansion, his fantastic parties, his cars, his clothes, his shirts. That incredible mountain of shirts that Gatsby is depicted as showing Daisy—"shirts of sheer linen and thick silk and fine flannel, . . . shirts with stripes and scrolls and plaids in coral and apple-green and lavender and faint orange, with monograms of Indian blue" (*GG*, p. 93)—is no less a manifestation of a kind of youthful self-aggrandizement than Nick's incredible collection of names of Gatsby's guests—"the Chester Beckers and the Leeches, and a man named Bunsen, . . . Doctor Webster Civet . . . and the Hornbeams and the Willie Voltaires, and a whole clan named Blackbuck" (*GG*, p. 61). Gatsby's intransigent faith in the face of Daisy's betrayal is no stronger than Nick's faith as expressed in his willful erasure of the obscene word from Gatsby's stoop. Nick's last words about our inevitable movement "back ceaselessly into the past" (*GG*, p. 182), his compulsion to tell Gatsby's story which is so much his own, his own final move back to the Midwest and "the thrilling returning trains of [his] youth" (*GG*, p. 177)—all make it clear that, at heart, Nick too believes that not only can one repeat the past; one inevitably has to. For Nick, Gatsby is clearly something "commensurate to his [Nick's] capacity for wonder" (*GG*, p. 182). His view of Gatsby has to be our view of him.

Nick appears both to see and not to see this truth about himself. His professed "unaffected scorn" for some aspects of Gatsby, his impatience with Gatsby's blindness to what Nick knows Daisy to be, his full awareness of Gatsby's underworld connections and shady, illegal dealings with Wolfsheim—all are nothing compared to that gorgeous "romantic readiness" that Nick attributes to Gatsby. This choice, this judgment, appears to be conscious enough on Nick's part, and one can hardly gainsay Gatsby's values when they are opposed to the "vast carelessness" of the Buchanans. But his final dismissal of even them—"I felt suddenly as though I were talking to a child" (*GG*, p. 181), his last judgment about Tom Buchanan— is perhaps indicative of an ultimate innocence of his own.

Additional evidence of Fitzgerald's distancing from Nick is provided by the intricate and elaborate series of parallels and doubles built into the structure of the novel. The relation of Nick to Gatsby has been the theme of most of what I have already said here about this novel; the relation of Fitzgerald to Nick is the implicit point toward which I am obviously moving. But many critics have seen others—Jordan is to Nick as Daisy is to Gatsby, Tom and Daisy as alter egos, and, most importantly, Myrtle Wilson as foil to Gatsby.

E. C. Bufkin makes a detailed and thorough examination of the Myrtle-Gatsby parallels.[27] Some of his points, if not necessarily his conclusions, are worthy of listing here: their similarities of "age, conduct, and social standing"; their almost absolutely mirrored relations to the Buchanans; the unrealistic "beau ideal" that Daisy and Tom represent for each; the happenstance that initially brought each pair together through the attraction of physical or material well-being; their mutual parties and self-improvement lists; and, of course, their finely balanced destruction by Tom and Daisy themselves. It may even be as significant as Bufkin makes it that Michaelis, who runs the coffee shop next door to Wilson's garage and sees the accident that kills Myrtle, tells the first policeman investigating her death that the car that struck her was "light green" (*GG*, p. 138) and thus for Bufkin establishes a link with Gatsby's nightly vigils staring at the "green light" on the end of Daisy's dock (*GG*, p. 22).

Bufkin gives several additional parallels, but this is enough surely to make the point that Fitzgerald is deliberately accenting the *sameness* of Myrtle and Gatsby. Yet Nick appears to see only their differences. His contrastive accounts of their deaths are giveaway enough. On the death of Myrtle he says, "Michaelis and this man reached her first, but when they had torn open her shirt waist, still damp with perspiration, they saw that her left breast was swinging loose like a flap. . . .

The mouth was wide open and ripped at the corners, as though she had choked a little in giving up the tremendous vitality she had stored so long" (*GG*, p. 138). But on that of Gatsby he says, "There was a faint, barely perceptible movement of the water as the fresh flow from one end urged its way toward the drain at the other. With little ripples that were hardly the shadows of waves, the laden mattress moved irregularly down the pool. A small gust of wind that scarcely corrugated the surface was enough to disturb its accidental course with its accidental burden. The touch of a cluster of leaves revolved it slowly, tracing, like the leg of transit, a thin red circle in the water" (*GG*, pp. 162–63). The cheap, the shoddy, the tawdry, and the grotesque characterize the first description; the elegiac and the sublime, the other. Dust and fertile water.

In the one scene in which Gatsby and Myrtle are literally brought together within Nick's ken, to repeat one of Bufkin's points, this is what we get:

> Gatsby has just told Nick, while they are riding in his "gorgeous car" [*GG*, pp. 63–68], a fantastic story about his life because "I don't want you to get the wrong idea of me from all these stories you hear." Then as they travel along, "the valley of ashes opened out on both sides of us," says Nick, "and I had a glimpse of Mrs. Wilson straining at the garage pump with panting vitality. . . ." The juxtaposition here creates a grim comic irony: Nick listens to pretentious Gatsby and sees Gatsby's double: what-is impinges upon what-is-said-to-be, both pumping.[28]

All *three* pumping, Bufkin might have said, for the corrective lesson appears to have been lost on Nick. The idea of Gatsby appeals irresistibly to some inner need of Nick's. His final choice is clear-cut. So, in its way, is Fitzgerald's—in his equally clear decision to present Nick's imperfect knowledge through his own demonstrably more convincing and richer knowledge. The question that remains is whether we also can choose—assimilate the opposed ideas *and* retain our ability to function. If not, perhaps nothing less than our own innocence is ultimately at stake. Jay Gatsby, in his way, perhaps did turn out all right in the end, as did, for Fitzgerald's intricate aesthetic purpose, Nick. It is that foul dust that floats in the wake of *our* dreams that remains—and that disturbs. And it is, finally, the question itself that is more important than the answer.

That question could be put in other terms: the extent to which imagination, for example, must be balanced with experience, the troublesome value of imagination when not so balanced, the perhaps unexpectedly intricate ways that they can be equated if perception is sufficiently keen and perspective sufficiently wide. Under this kind of rubric *The Sun Also Rises* is a much narrower book, the relation of imagination to experience not consciously so central, experience breaking through and disrupting imagination almost in spite of itself. Although one might be tempted to say of Benjy in *The Sound and the Fury* that it is a case of imagination *creating* experience, the truth is precisely the opposite: experience creates imagination—not only creates it but carefully nurtures and continuously monitors it. Indeed, so true is this for Faulkner that it provides one explanation for an artistic virtuosity (in scope and scale) in subsequent works that is greater than that of either Hemingway (who never clearly recognized the problem) or Fitzgerald (who could never satisfactorily resolve it).

But at one fine point, perhaps, all three of these works adhere very closely. "A useful and deliberate innocence," says Hoffman, is "the great strength of the decade," the precise phrase wherein "the positive values of the 1920's may be suggested." Hoffman's eloquent overall concern with this concept is much wider than the specific concern here with three innocent narrators, and his own uses of the word *innocence* are much broader than the specialized application of it in this essay. At one point, however, there is agreement. "To begin with the 'new' [Hoffman is explaining a pervasive methodology of the 1920s] is to begin innocently afresh, to explore 'the thing seen' in terms of the 'way it is seen.'" His critical subject, he suggests a few sentences later, is precisely how "the writers of the 1920's . . . had both to *see* a world as it frankly was and to *re-establish* that world in their literary formulations."[29] His subject, hence, has become in a way my discovered method; his method, in still another way, my recovered subject. The result is meaningful replication, echoes everywhere.

But let us reformulate one final time—and somewhat playfully. The last of these innocent narrators, Nick Carraway, is in time (1925) the first. We are thus both at a beginning and at an end, and with an answer I somewhat only half-perversely describe as a question. The end is my beginning: Faulkner's Benjy of 1929 with an idiot's mind arrested in stasis at the moment of birth. Hemingway's Jake Barnes is a regression *and* progression, the perennial adolescent just on the edge of shedding, but neatly and appropriately floating in between. Nick Carraway is no child, yet he returns to his childhood home to construct a tale of a monumental innocence, which Fitzgerald contrived to test our own. Borne backward, we come forward; striving forward, we are borne ceaselessly back into the past. The beginning is surely no end. But this ending, it is hoped, might just be a small beginning.

FOUR

The Obverse Relation

Some Western Flights Eastward (in Literature and Film)

I WAS ORIGINALLY led to what I am here calling the obverse relation in fiction and film by a lifelong fascination with movie Westerns, on the one hand, and at least a half-lifetime of interest in the fiction of Henry James, on the other—a coupling which, on the face of it, was not very predictable, a coupling, at any rate, initially surprising to me.

The Jamesian contribution to this obverse relation is, of course, hardly surprising to anyone. Most students of American culture are aware of the post–Civil War movement of some Americans to look to Europe in search of their past, their history, and a cultural enrichment and a quality of experience they deemed it impossible to find in an expansive, aggressive America. This movement to the East was surely as much a historical fact of the age as America's concomitant and simultaneous move in the other direction—toward a new industrialization, toward new land and a new frontier west of the Mississippi, toward, in short, the future: *Turn West, Turn East*, Mark Twain *and* Henry James, the historical simultaneity of American turns westward *and* eastward, as Henry Seidel Canby saw in 1951. But even a very early book of Twain's was entitled *The Innocents Abroad*, and two of James's earliest and most well-known generic portraits, Christopher Newman and Daisy Miller, have frequently been said to be portraits of westerners. (That Whitman's "passage to India" is literally a move westward that becomes ultimately "eastern," circle fashion, is too confusing a complication of directional signals that are already complicated enough, although my own last example also involves a departure that becomes a return.) Henry James's thrust eastward, however, his role as chronicler of what I am calling here the obverse relation, is well known, obvious, and, I assume, accepted.

The manifestation of this phenomenon in the movie Western perhaps is not. At any rate, it was originally not apparent to me. I suspect, in fact, that my lifelong attraction to the Western, at least until quite recently, had been primarily a visceral attraction merely to the exotically scenic, on the one hand, and to its seemingly simplistic formulas (good guys versus bad, whites versus redmen, ranchers versus rustlers, settlers versus ranchers), on the other—in brief, the attraction of instant violence amid scenes of idyllic or pastoral magnificence. Whatever the reasons, my love affair with the Western has been a long and intense one.

In 1969 mere happenstance brought that popular mod-Western *Easy Rider* to Lafayette, Indiana, at a time when I was immersed in some academic work on Christopher Newman of James's *The American*. It was that literary/cinematic joining of an "eastering" experience by some American westerners that led me, first, to find analogies in Twain and Hemingway and then to see, somewhat more intricately I believe, some extensions of that theme in an unlikely context, films from Italy, Bernardo Bertolucci's *Last Tango in Paris* and Sergio Leone's *Once upon a Time in the West.*

An "Easy Ride" for Henry James

Given my already described background and context, my discoveries on first viewing *Easy Rider* should not surprise. What I of course saw in that film were the trials and tribulations of James's Christopher Newman. Although his part was split between two characters, Wyatt or Captain America, dressed in red, white, and blue crash helmet and leather jacket (Peter Fonda), and Billy the Kid, who wore a Kit Carson fringed jacket and bush hat (Dennis Hopper), it was Christopher Newman, all the same. And it was a Christopher Newman coming from the same sort of vision meeting the same sort of end for the same sort of reasons.

The melodramatic plot of *The American* is an intricate one. In 1868, Christopher Newman, an enormously rich middle-aged American, comes to Paris to discover some splendid sequel to his achieved ability to make money. His plans are to "do" Europe and perhaps to find, in some supreme product of old-world civilization, the perfect wife. Through a mutual acquaintance, Newman is introduced to Claire de Cintré, a young widow of noble birth, who strikes the American as precisely the woman he would like to marry. Upon first calling at her home, however, he is turned away by her haughty elder brother, Urbain de Bellegarde. After a summer of traveling in Europe, Newman discovers the Bellegardes now willing to receive him, and he soon meets other members of the family: Urbain's wife; the charming younger brother Valentin; the shrewd and proud old Marquise, Madame de Bellegarde; and a servant, the sympathetic old Englishwoman Mrs. Bread. Newman becomes a close friend of Valentin, who encourages Newman's courtship of his sister. Urbain and his mother, however, tolerate him only because of his immense wealth. But Claire finally accepts his proposal, the engagement is formally announced, and the Marquis reluctantly introduces Newman to his aristocratic friends. Meanwhile the American has come to know Mlle. Noémie Nioche, a copyist of paintings, whose weak-willed father becomes Newman's French teacher. Newman is generous to Noémie and eventually introduces her to Valentin, who immediately becomes infatuated. Through Newman's generosity, she is able to give up her painting, leaves her father's rooms, and becomes an apparently successful courtesan. Although Valentin clearly sees her for what she is, he continues to visit her. Ultimately she is the cause of a duel in which the young Frenchman is fatally wounded. Before learning of the outcome of the duel, however, Newman is summoned by the Bellegardes and told that his marriage is off. Unwilling at the last moment to accept a "commercial person" and hoping for a more aristocratic match with a Lord Deepmere, they have demanded that Claire break her engagement. Before Newman can confront Claire alone, he is called to Valentin's death bed. Guessing what has happened, Valentin expresses his shame at his family's action and reveals to Newman that Mrs. Bread knows a guilty secret about the family which the American may use to further his own ends. After Valentin's funeral, Claire tells Newman of her decision to enter a convent. He thereupon seeks out Mrs. Bread and acquires from her proof that the old Marquise had murdered her husband. Newman threatens to expose them, but they still refuse to allow the marriage. Although determined at first to fulfill his revenge, Newman cannot bring himself to reveal the Bellegardes' secret. After months of brooding and melancholy travel, he discovers that Claire has indeed taken the veil of a nun, and he destroys the evidence of the murder.

No less melodramatic but perhaps somewhat less intricate, *Easy Rider* begins with Wyatt and Billy also sufficiently rich. Having just sold a large supply of dope to a wealthy pusher on the West Coast, they take off across the Southwest with

their money safely concealed in the tanks of their motor-
cycles. Their direction is vaguely eastward, toward New Orleans in time for Mardi Gras, and perhaps on to Florida.
Along the way, they camp outdoors, smoking marijuana each
night until asleep. They stop at a ranch to repair their bikes,
have a meal with the family there, pick up a hitchhiker, and
accompany him to the commune where he lives. Despite the
friendliness of the commune dwellers and a refreshing swim
there with two naked girls, Billy is eager to leave, and they
again take to the road. In a small Texas town, they are arrested for their cycling antics. In the town jail they meet an
alcoholic civil-rights lawyer, George Hanson, who secures
their release and persuades them to let him join them. They
get along well together, and Hanson discovers he likes pot as
well as he does booze. One night, however, following an al-
tercation earlier in the day brought on by the hostility and
bigotry of the local patrons in a luncheonette where they had
stopped to eat, they are set upon by a group of "vigilantes"
who pummel Hanson to death and leave Wyatt and Billy
badly bruised and bleeding. The two riders continue on to
New Orleans, visit a whorehouse there that Hanson had
known, have a bad LSD "trip" in a local cemetery, and mo-
rosely ride on toward Florida. In or near the Florida pan-
handle, they are passed by two rednecks in a pickup truck
who, incensed at their long hair, provoke an exchange of
obscene insults and blast the two riders with a shotgun.

These two works are totally unalike, yet so remarkably
similar. The names, for example, are clearly generic American names: Christopher Newman and Captain America (even
when the latter is qualified as Wyatt or Billy). Both of their
backgrounds are clearly defined as western ones, although
Newman's is more murkily so. But Newman's huge fortune
is defined as having come from the West, where he is described as having "sat with western humorists in circles
around cast-iron stoves and had seen tall stories grow taller
without toppling over." Constance Rourke saw years ago how
the imprecise timing of the book made Newman's adventures
there coincide with the period of the Great Gold Rush (in her
American Humor: A Study of the National Character). Newman had also been, we are told, one of the youngest generals
in the Union army. He had also apparently been, among
other things, a manufacturer of washtubs. The point is that

he was very rich, and the source of his fortune is as open to question as is Captain America's cashing in on a huge cache of cocaine.

Newman's journey eastward to Europe to fulfill his vision of a better life is also paralleled in Wyatt and Billy's ride toward Florida. The tarnish Newman found instead embedded in the Bellegardes is not radically different from what the "easy riders" would themselves have found, had they arrived on Florida's Gold Coast. Their motives are clearly the same—as is the underlying knowledge of their creators of what *had* to be at the end of their rainbows.

The next parallel is in their confrontations with established and intransigent societies, which view them and their dreams as anathema. The rednecks in *Easy Rider* react almost precisely as do the Bellegardes. Moreover, when members of those established societies react favorably to the tone and style and "moves" of these voyagers (as does Valentin in the novel and the drunken George Hanson [Jack Nicholson] in the film), they of course must be destroyed. And they are. Valentin's involvement with Newman leads to his involvement with Noémie Nioche, the direct cause of his death by duel at the hand of the gross German beer baron. Hanson's involvement with Wyatt and Billy is even more directly the cause of his head being smashed in with an ax handle brutally wielded by local bigots.

What attracts these two rebels to these two visionaries is perhaps more significant than their parallel fates. For Valentin, Newman possesses "something," he says, "it worries me to have missed." Quickly specifying, Valentin continues: "It's not money, it's not even brains, though evidently yours have been excellent for your purpose. It's not your superfluous stature, though I should have rather liked to be a couple of inches taller. It's a sort of air you have of being imperturbably, being irremovably and indestructibly (that's the thing) at home in the world.... You strike me ... as a man who stands about at his ease and looks straight over ever so many high walls." In the most famous of the many descriptions of Newman in the novel he concludes: "I seem to see you move everywhere like a big stockholder on his favorite railroad. You make me feel awfully my want of shares." Newman's air of being "at home in the world," his leg stretching, his easy moves "like a big stockholder on his favorite railroad"—these are Newman's great attractions to Valentin, those which made him "feel" so "awfully" his "want of shares." His suffocating closeness to his domineering mother, the old marquise, and his relationship to the stiflingly correct and urbane Urbaine de Bellegarde, of course, are also at play. Hanson's family is also reported as being suffocatingly restrictive. The appeal of the easy riders is surely the appeal of their apparently easy moves; the momentary euphoria of their proffered and accepted "grass" to Hanson is no more than a modern updating of Newman's appeal to Valentin. E-A-Z-Z-Y movement is obviously the attraction; E-A-Z-Z-Y Rider precisely the giveaway.

The end of all of these American dreamers is, of course, failure. Wyatt's explanation (in a line most viewers remember) is much more direct than Newman's: "We blew it!" Even the idyllic commune sequence does not redeem the sense of failure. Fonda later stated that he felt that the commune sequence is the weakest in the movie and that the one line he now wishes were not in the film is the one about the commune dwellers: "They're gonna make it" (as quoted in Elizabeth Campbell's "Rolling Stone Raps with Peter Fonda"). "We blew it," Wyatt says, and they in turn are blown to hell.

Newman's failure is much more complicated. He is not literally dead—in spite of his visits to the Rue d'Enfer. Many have seen him emerging as victorious. But he literally *fails* to get the girl. He *fails* to exact his revenge. He *fails* even to understand his own limitations. But his limitations are there as clearly as Wyatt's articulated awareness of his and Billy's, and these limitations are meant to be for these visionaries as much the cause of their defeats as are the rigidities of the two societies they affront.

Captain America *is* Christopher Newman.

All of which is not to say—or even to suggest—that Dennis Hopper is Henry James. It is not even to suggest that Hopper has read James, although Terry Southern, who also contributed to the script, may well have. Nor is it to suggest a necessary knowledge of or familiarity with the two twentieth-century novels so often seen as extensive parallels to *The American*: Fitzgerald's *The Great Gatsby* (itself, of course, a Western of sorts in the obverse role) and Faulkner's *Absalom, Absalom!* What I want to suggest instead is simply a simultaneity of vision—a Henry James novel of 1876 and a Dennis

Hopper film of 1969 expressing a single cultural idea: the westerner, fattened (and thus both enabled and possibly corrupted) by western spoils, turning eastward in quest of that "something commensurate" to "his capacity for wonder," as Fitzgerald has Nick Carraway so much better express the westering vision in *Gatsby*.

Eastering Westerns:
Mark Twain and Hemingway

Reformulations of the westering experience in a European setting can also be approached through James's great contemporary Mark Twain. Hank Morgan, Twain's Connecticut Yankee, is, to be sure, more nineteenth-century journeyman and entrepreneur than cowboy, his mythical flight backward and eastward to sixth-century Camelot more a flight back to childhood than to Europe. But Morgan is also a westerner, born "just over the river, in the country," and part of his quest is to empty the saddles of their childhood burdens of the curse of knight-errantry. This he accomplishes in a man-to-man showdown, first with lasso against lance. The conclusion is as predictable as that in any "oater": "I was sitting my horse at ease, and swinging the great loop of my lasso in wide circles about my head; the moment he was under way, I started for him; when the space between us had narrowed to forty feet, I sent the snaky spirals of the rope a-cleaving through the air, then darted aside and faced about and brought my trained animal to halt with all his feet braced under him for the surge. The next moment the rope sprang taut and yanked Sir Sagramor out of the saddle: Great Scott, but there was a sensation!" He similarly disposes of five additional challengers, including the great Sir Launcelot, which finally provokes Merlin to steal Hank's rope. Then the "cowboy business" (as Twain calls it) is transformed into a more deadly six-shooter business. The second conclusion is also predictable, even with five hundred knights "scrambling into their saddles, and . . . clattering down upon" Hank with his twin guns ablazing: "Bang! One saddle empty. Bang! another one. Bang—Bang! And . . . he banged two." Nine of his available twelve shots hit home. Hank "raised both revolvers and pointed them— the halted host stood their ground just about one good square moment, then broke and fled." The conclusion of the book, however (albeit also foregone), is not victory—but failure once again (as with Newman, as with Captain America) when two-gun Hank electrocutes, dynamites, machine guns, and drowns a host of twenty-five thousand of England's finest. In the end the victors themselves are entombed by the mounting bodies of those they have killed; they who have conquered are, in turn, conquered. Failure. The western dream also fails in this eastern past.

My other example in this pair is somewhat less direct, somewhat less explicit, but nonetheless follows Twain's example obviously enough: Hemingway's flight east to Europe in multiple quest of new frontiers.

Not until Hemingway died did we begin to see how his moves eastward were so characteristically American quests for the American West—not, that is, until we began to see *A Moveable Feast, Death in the Afternoon,* and *Green Hills of Africa* as a trilogy of successive quests for the frontier dream. (Cuba, to be sure, was a fourth; Idaho, ironically the "real" West, was a fifth—even if this last, more ironic still, was a retreat, a retreat, moreover, to what was by then only a "token" West.) Robert Stephens, whose book *Hemingway's Non-fiction* (1968) I am following here, makes a more than ample case for this view of Hemingway's moves. He follows Cowley in seeing Paris (for the expatriates of the 1920s) as "the newer prairie of the mind," a "grazing area" is Stephens's phrase, that "both fed and poisoned Hemingway and his friends." But "the frontier, like art," Stephens continues, "involved change as well as continuity, variety as well as pattern," and thus became also "a place to outgrow."

Spain as American frontier is even more directly seen, with the "hills and plateaus of Castile, Aragon, and Andalusia" almost always for Hemingway "the mountains of Wyoming and Montana," the "forest of the Irati . . . always that forest remembered from childhood, whether . . . real in Michigan or remembered from books." Moreover, of course, there were the wild, free-ranging bulls, "branded and tested on the range as were American range cattle." But more important, says Stephens, was the link of the bulls to the primal past, a link of "primeval strength kept intact well into the twentieth century." Hemingway's well-known aesthetic of the kill is not mentioned by Stephens in this context, although it might have been, for Hemingway's somewhat sensational contention that "true enjoyment of killing . . . makes the great matador," that "feeling of rebellion against death which comes from its administering," one of those "God-like attributes" of giving death as a way of rebelling against it, can also be seen as a manifestation of the frontier mystique. It is not at any rate inconsistent with D. H. Lawrence's famous (or notorious) elaboration of that mystique in his description of Natty Bumppo as an "isolate, almost selfless, stoic . . . who lives by death, by killing." But Stephens is also ultimately right in his contention that Spain "was a frontier also to outgrow," for "bullfighting was finally an institution that corrupted many men and because Spanish governments altered mountains and rivers."

It was, however, the African hunt that became the most explicitly "American" of Hemingway's many sojourns, as many readers have noticed. The terrain there, as in Spain, was everywhere identifiable to him as the American West. Moreover, it was a hunter's terrain, just as the American West had been to Hemingway a hunter's West. That Africa was the oldest of continents at the same time that it was the newest of New Worlds reflected for him the appeal that the primal was always to exert: it still retained the possibility of becoming more than America had become. No wonder, then, that Africa becomes an almost idyllic setting for his ubiquitous ruminations on the craft of writing, especially American writing, on America itself, on the narrator as American writer, and on his life against an American background.

This is not the place for an analysis of the development in Hemingway's aesthetic that coincided with the African experience, except insofar as to say that he gained a perspective about himself that was in some ways the most regenerative in his career. The perspective gained, moreover, is explicitly tied to the frontier ideal, even as it was built into the structure of the book. For the "story" of *Green Hills of Africa* is not of results but of processes, of how kinds of failures are transformed into kinds of triumphs (not in itself, of course, anything new). But the new catalyst throughout here is memory—and the variety of ways it becomes the transforming principle of any act's essence, that of the hunter no less than that of the artist. The hunter's multiple failures in *Green Hills* (Sheridan Baker in his *Ernest Hemingway: An Introduction and Interpretation* [1967] has a fine list of the variety of ways that the narrator comes in second best) become the writer's successes through memory—through memory of his personal past, his larger historical past, and, in this book in particular, his cultural past, his reading. Thus, the pursuit of the book's active action—the pursuit of game on the first level, that of self and of others on the next, and only finally, perhaps, that of language itself—becomes the end. Pursuit *is* the end, not merely the means, although it is that too. All of which the very subheads themselves clearly state: "Pursuit and Conversation," "Pursuit Remembered," "Pursuit and Failure," "Pursuit as Happiness."

Hence, the famous idyllic calm near the end of *Green Hills* flows, for at least a time, from the rediscovered, the *remembered* American West:

> A continent ages quickly once we come. The natives live in harmony with it. But the foreigner destroys, cuts down the trees, drains the water, so that the water supply is altered and in a short time the soil, once the sod is turned under, is cropped out and, next, it starts to blow away. . . . [But] I would come back to Africa but not to make a living from it. . . . But I would come back to where it pleased me to live; to really live. Not just let my life pass. Our people went to America because that was the place to go then. It had been a good country and we had made a bloody mess of it and I would go, now, somewhere else as we had always had the right to go somewhere else and as we had always gone. . . . Let others come to America who did not know that they had come too late. . . . Now I would go somewhere else. We always went in the old days and there were still good places to go. I knew a good country when I saw one. Here there was game, plenty of birds, and I liked the natives. Here I could shoot and fish. That, and writing, and reading, and seeing pictures was all I cared about doing. And I could remember all the pictures.

But Africa as frontier was not to endure either. Hence, Hemingway's brief return to Cuba and its central image of the Gulf Stream—"his long-used stream-flowing-into-the-sea-metaphor for time and timelessness" (to use Stephens's phrase)—perhaps presaged a more healthy turn eastward, even as the Gulf Stream runs north and east to join the Atlantic drift. Thus, the final literal return, against the grain, to the real West of Idaho becomes, perhaps inevitably, suicidal. Failure again.

Westering Europeans

My last two examples are both films, European films, moreover, which appropriate western American myths for their own modern European needs. One is a sort of political allegory that is viciously critical of the eastward-moving American and his havoc-spreading corruption; the other is a lovingly sustained, if gently parodic, rerendering of the "Western" in classic form. Bernardo Bertolucci's *Last Tango in Paris* and Sergio Leone's *Once upon a Time in the West* form an odd couple—but perhaps no more odd than that formed by Captain America and Christopher Newman, my first pair.

At any rate, it is again Henry James who is the logical referent, although Twain's Hank Morgan could also be used (as one of his innocents abroad), as could Hemingway (in his moves to Paris, Spain, and Africa as quests for new American frontiers) or perhaps any number of other native chroniclers of Americans in Europe, from Scott Fitzgerald to James Baldwin. But it is Henry James who works best here as a referent for viewing what was surely the most widely discussed movie of 1973. For whatever else that controversial movie is, it is also an international fable in the Jamesian mode—an American in Paris (a Christopher Newman or a Lambert Strether) attempting to fulfill his American destiny. That Paul (Marlon Brando) is meant to be a generic American is unmistakable—his midwestern farm background replete with cow-dung on his shoes; his varied vocations as boxer, actor, bongo player, and revolutionary. Who but a *Moby-Dick*-raised American would be "whale-fucking in the Congo," as Paul so delicately puts it? Jeanne (Maria Schneider) is equally generic; she is Paris and also, therefore, Europe. Nothing is more pervasive in James than the coupling of America with Europe.

The plot of this profoundly satisfying film is much too intricate to give here in detail. Paul's chance encounter with
Jeanne while they are both looking at a vacant apartment,
their repeated sexual gyrations there following the mysterious suicide of Paul's wife Rosa (Veronica Lazare) and preceding Jeanne's planned marriage to the young film director
Tom (Jean-Pierre Leaud), their temporary decision not to reveal to one another their names, the eventual revelation of
Paul's and some of Jeanne's past notwithstanding, the bizarre
sketch of Paul confronting the embalmed corpse of his wife,
the unforgettable tango scene, Paul's drunken, pitiful, and
futile attempt to persuade Jeanne to marry him, and her
reply with a bullet from her father's pistol—all does scant
justice to this international encounter between a young European and a middle-aged American.

Bertolucci, an admitted Freudian and Marxist, gives us,
however, a delightful twist to this international fable. He
reverses the normal Jamesian stance, expropriating an
American-made myth to serve what he apparently considers
to be his modern European aesthetic and political needs. In
the current world, Bertolucci seems to be saying, the American is the old, corrupt, and corrupting, just as the European
so often is in James. Europe's possibilities for rebirth and
growth, for at least regeneration, according to Bertolucci, are
absolutely and specifically dependent upon the destruction of
America—an America, as personified by Paul, still holding
on to its bourgeois values, its protestations to the contrary
notwithstanding; a commercial America, half-proprietor of a
whorehouse in Paris; a deluded America that thinks its forty-
five-year-old, gum-chewing men can retreat to the French
countryside for a new life with nineteen-year-old French
girls; a drunken and defiant America, baring its lower back-
side to a scandalized and stylized Europe; an America, finally,
which openly acknowledges its contemporary role as inheritor of European colonialism. Paul's penultimate line (while
wearing the French colonial hat of Jeanne's father) is, "I ran
through Africa, Asia, and Indonesia, and now I've found you."

Europe, therefore, from Bertolucci's point of view, has not
one wisp of a chance in such a world. Modern America (or at
least its residue as represented by Paul) must be destroyed—
and is. "I don't know his name," concludes Jeanne after she
shoots him. "I don't know who he is, he tried to rape me, he's

a madman. I don't know his name." But James would have known it. So would have Twain, Fitzgerald, Hemingway, and, among many others, even Theodore Dreiser. And so, I think, do we. However variously it has been and was to be spelled, it all comes out in the end as the American.

Another of the movie's modes, the carefully orchestrated regression of Paul from manhood to fetus, from a kind of at least relatively honest and questing experience at the beginning back and down at the end to an outrageously destructive innocence, would also have been recognized by almost any chronicler of the American flight eastward. For a destructive innocence is right at the core of a whole literary movement in America: from Clyde Griffith to Jay Gatsby; from Robert Jordan to Hank Morgan; from Christopher Newman, Daisy Miller, and Isabel Archer to Captain America. *Last Tango* is a very "literary" film, and nowhere more so than in its eastering Jamesian modes.[1]

But if for Bertolucci modern America must be destroyed, for Bertolucci's compatriot Sergio Leone an earlier America, a specifically western America, must also be resurrected (and perhaps even for Bertolucci himself, who is listed in the credits as having contributed to the script of *Once upon a Time in the West*).

Once upon a Time is of course a special case and fits into my scheme here only in a very special way. Its elegiac quality first occurred to me when I viewed it during the same week that I saw *Butch Cassidy and the Sundance Kid*, one of the first and certainly one of the best and most popular of the end-the-Western Westerns. I remember thinking at the time that *Butch Cassidy* is not the end of the Western; *Once upon a Time* is, if indeed it is to be ended, just as *Don Quixote* was the end of the chivalric romance. They are lovingly both satirical pokes at established traditions and genres at the same time that they beautifully fulfill the intrinsic aspirations of those traditions. Indeed, after them further attempts are unnecessary.

Cervantes came to the tradition of knight-errantry late in its development (as did Leone to the Western). Moreover, he drew on a seemingly inexhaustible supply of childhood memories of knights in shining armor (as Leone has told us he drew on the innumerable Hollywood Westerns he viewed in his youth). Finally, he made it his own only because the tradition he was commemorating could be aesthetically distanced because it originally flourished much earlier in France as well as in Spain (much as the Hollywood Western and the Japanese Akira Kurosawa provided a useful perspective for the Italian Leone). Extreme though this no doubt is, I believed then—and I think I believe now—that *Once upon a Time in the West* is the *Don Quixote* of the Western.

This apparent diversion brings me back to my central issue: *Once upon a Time in the West* as the ultimate western flight eastward, the fateful past of the Western commemorated, to be sure (about which more in a minute), but also corrected and resurrected as therapeutic memory by and for a modern world.

The film opens at a remote railroad depot with three marvelous murderous henchmen (Jack Elam, Woody Strode, and a knuckle-popping third) lying in ambush for the Man, who remains unnamed (Charles Bronson), whose mysterious trademark is that he plays sad songs on a harmonica. The Man guesses their murderous intent when they refuse to answer questions about a character named Frank and shoots all three before they can reach for their guns. The scene shifts to the isolated desert ranch house, where McBain, a huge, vibrant Irishman is preparing an outdoor feast with his three motherless children in anticipation of the arrival of Jill (Claudia Cardinale), a New Orleans whore whom he has recently and secretly married. Shots again ring out as Frank (played by Henry Fonda) and his duster-garbed gang gun down McBain and his three children, then plant evidence implicating Cheyenne, a local, notorious half-breed outlaw played by Jason Robards. Jill arrives at the ranch to discover the McBain funeral in progress. She later learns that McBain's promise of future wealth awaited the day when the railroad passed through his property because of its water hole and the inevitable rise there of a thriving community. In spite of the Man's protection, Jill is finally sufficiently frightened, following her rapelike seduction by Frank, to auction off her property. The Man, it turns out, has a mysterious vendetta with Frank, who is in the employ of a crippled railway executive named Morton (played by Gabriele Ferzetti), who covets McBain's land for its potential value as part of his compulsive drive to extend his railroad to the Pacific. Through additional intricacies too complex to relate here, the auction is foiled by the Man, and Sweetwater is returned to Jill; Cheyenne kills off Morton (though he himself is fatally wounded in doing so); and Frank shows up for the inevitable shoot-out with the Man. The Man, of course, is the faster gun. Not until after he is shot, but before he dies, does Frank learn the reason for the Man's vendetta: when he was only fifteen, Frank had forced him to play the harmonica as Frank tortured and hanged his brother. His brother avenged, the Man says good-bye to Jill and rides off, the wounded Cheyenne joining him a moment later only to drop from his horse and die from his wounds. The movie's final shot is of Bronson moving away, the dead body of Cheyenne draped over the horse behind him, and the train chugging into the settlement as Jill distributes water to the workmen. The title comes whirling out of the distance and aligns itself on the screen: *Once upon a Time in the West.*

The elements of the traditional Western are apparent enough even in the uneasy clumsiness of this truncated summary: the confrontation of frontier and civilization (water hole and train); white hat and black hat, and mediating gray-hat (Robards); long-suffering whore transformed into sustenance-giving and civilizing fertility figure who does *not* get her man; ruthless railroad magnate who buys men as if they were five-cent beers; soft-spoken gun-toter on a mysterious quest for revenge (but also cowboy as musician); shoot-outs by the wagon-load of every kind imaginable (trick-shooting through the toe of Cheyenne's boot, brutal face-forward blasting of children, the super-fast draw on three professional baddies, the moving-target shot at men on horseback, the storefront shoot-out, the last, adagio-paced two-man confrontation of hero and villain); and, finally, of course, magnificently expansive scenery, rugged and picturesque.

Treatment, however, is more significant in a way than subject, although subject, as I hope to show in a moment, is perhaps somewhat more complex than I have yet suggested.

Pacing best reveals the underlying *hommage* of the film, the expansive pacing of the photography no less than of the action, with sustained close-ups (the camera focuses for what seems to be minutes on *one* of Charles Bronson's eyes during his shoot-out with Fonda) and equally sustained long-shots. These are interspersed with explosive cuts from scene to scene, usually accompanied, moreover, by explosive sound—railroad noises in one instance, the fluttering of quail in another, and everywhere in the background the hauntingly insistent and indelibly romantic musical score by Ennio Morricone, it too alternating the harmonica solos *pianissimo* with full orchestra *fortissimo*. Action is always slow motioned, ballet-like, ceremonial—from the comic preamble of Jack Elam's bemused somnolence at the buzz of a caught fly in the barrel of his six-gun through the slow-moving dance (Julian Smith, in a paper on Leone's film to which I am much indebted, has called it "The Last Tango in Sweetwater"[2]) of the final shoot-out.

Hommage also pervades the film in still other ways—some more explicit, some perhaps less so. John Ford, of course, is there in Jill's unforgettable buggy ride through Monument Valley no less than in the plot's ties to Ford's 1924 classic, *The Iron Horse*, and its treatment of national progress as balanced by a son's search for his father's killer. Even the harmonica-playing hero has antecedents of sorts in the tradition of the singing cowboy, although Gene Autry and Tex Ritter are far removed from the tone of this movie. But hommage is here, too, simply in the hyperbole (always balanced on the fine thin line of loving parody), in the ubiquitous hyperbole of Western plots and characters, as already suggested, but also in the hyperbole of shapes and varieties of greed, of revenge, and of ambition: "doubles crosses and betrayals by the handful," as Smith has listed them, "deaths by the score, and one of the biggest sets ever built (on a hundred acres in Spain, [with] saloons, hotels, depots, stables, houses, banks, stores—some abuilding, some already run down)—and five miles of track . . . and more big names in big roles than half a dozen lesser films." But the small elements are no less important, and the central Western theme of the transcontinental ambitions of a railroad builder versus the desire of one man to avenge his brother's murder is here made not only through loving care, but also through comic distance, casting, color, music, architecture, and balletic movement: all cohering in the finest tribute ever made to the Western.

But *Once upon a Time in the West* is, finally, also a modern Western, a modern document, the product of a modern sensibility. For what Leone has also done in this film is to catch a historical moment (the joining of the mechanical and the natural, of railroad and water). (I pass over the obviously

mod touches: the explicit sex and language, the visual violence, the sweet-sad, mod-old harmonica playing, the sophisticated camera work, the stills, the slow motion, the brilliant
cuts.) The ostensible villain, Morton, is seen to be no less a
visionary than McBain, his dream of the blue Pacific explicitly tied to McBain's dreams for his station. The crippled
nature of Morton's vision (as indicated by his creeping tuber-
culosis) is no less insistently indicated than is the nature of
McBain's in his secret marriage to the whore. They both die
violently, moreover, and significantly by mud hole and by
well; McBain's small-scale model of his town is duplicated by
that of Morton's on his train. Yet, the necessary joining, the
interdependence, of rail and water, of the natural *and* the
mechanical, is also Leone's point, the suggestive thrust of his
first scene (by water tank and rail stop)-no less than that of
his last (of water bearer and railroad workers). This is the
film's realistically modern hope—as resurrected from America's legendary past; the mechanical and the natural in happy
and productive conjunction, the former not to be manipulated
for private greed and self-aggrandizement, the latter not to
be possessed for private profit. The loving legend of good guy
and bad and all in between is here reversed as somewhere
once upon a time out of the West, we *now* see, in one of the
inspirations of Leone's casting: the lowly Chicano (Bronson)
is the hero; the rugged Wasp (Fonda), the villain.

Too pat, too didactic, even too Marxist? Perhaps. But what
fun, nevertheless. And as the most extreme example of my
medley, my admitted miscellany, of eastering Westerns, it is
also, paradoxically, my most *western* Western. It could not, at
any rate, have been made by an American, its occasional
American scenes (in Utah and Arizona), its predominantly
American cast, its dependence on American money notwithstanding.

Distance is crucial to its achievement—its beautiful elegiac tone of remote familiarity. *Once upon a Time in the West*
thrives on the old possibility, thrives because it is old, is
distant, is remote, but thrives too because it is also new and
fresh and vivid. It contains that at which we laugh and
mourn, which we hold and disdain, which we ceremoniously
memorialize and contemporaneously acknowledge. Distance
is also crucial in making intelligible those other dichotomies
that I have tried to formulate in this context: the particular

ambiguity of the possible and the corrupt (as in James and Dennis Hopper), the ultimately failed transplanted westering idea in older and eastering European climes (as in Twain and Hemingway), and even in the inversion that transforms the ideology (as in *Last Tango in Paris*).

Those who have attempted to move the Western eastward in less distant, more direct ways—*Coogan's Bluff, McCloud, Midnight Cowboy*, and, more symbolically still, *Taxi Driver*, Peckinpah's move to Cornwall (in *Straw Dogs*), and John Wayne's even more eastering move to Viet Nam (in *The Green Berets*)—have, finally, at least comparatively, moved us not at all. (A possible startling exception to these *failed* eastward-moving Westerns might well be the 1978 film *The Deer Hunter*. Its modern, audaciously "eastern" settings, an all-too-mythical Pennsylvania steel town [deliberately named "Clairton"] and an all-too-realistic Viet Nam as appropriate terrain for a modern-day Natty Bumppo, the "westerner" seen as a son or perhaps grandson of Russian immigrants— all struck me as conceivably carrying the modes of my obverse relation far beyond anything I could have originally imagined.) But within what I could then imagine, it was the Italian Leone, as Smith said so eloquently, who most beautifully brings us "home to the West—brings us home because he is not of the West, appropriately rediscovering the modern possibility in that land first discovered by one of his ancient compatriots and named after another." Whatever else appears in this mode, the remote familiarity of *Once upon a Time in the West* will remain a challenging act to follow.

FIVE

The Black/White Continuum

Some Recent Examples in Bellow, Malamud, and Updike

IN THE OPENING pages of Saul Bellow's *Mr. Sammler's Planet* the protagonist is musing over the effect on him of having witnessed on a New York City bus a tall, handsome, elegantly garbed black pickpocket ply his trade between Columbus Circle and 72nd Street. With some reluctance, Sammler accepts his admitted fascination with the sight and his compulsion to rewitness the performance, even if he is somewhat apprehensive that the pickpocket has spotted him. He reports that "four fascinating times he had watched the thing done" (p. 10).[1] Although he can say that "he didn't give a damn for the glamour, the style, the art of criminals" (he had little use "for the romance of the outlaw" [p. 11]), he nonetheless "wanted very much to see the thing again. . . . He craved a repetition" (p. 11). Speculating over the reason for this craving, he recalls the explicitness with which he could remember the details of how Dostoevski's Raskolnikov "brought down the ax on the bare head of the old woman" (p. 11) and is thus led to say that, yes, "horror, crime, murder, did vivify all the phenomena, the most ordinary details of experience" (p. 11), that "in evil as in art there was illumination" (p. 11). He receives from the sight of the crime, he somewhat pontifically concludes (his intentions to go to the police notwithstanding), "the benefit of an enlarged vision. The air was (somehow) brighter. The world . . . was wickedly lighted up . . . all objects . . . explicit" and with an "explicitness [that] taunted Mr. Minutely-Observant Artur Sammler." "All metaphysicians," Sammler exhorts his imaginary listener, "please take note. Here is how it is. You will never see more clearly. . . . What do you make of it?" (p. 12). But what Sammler then literally makes out is simply a vandalized public phone booth, its floor "smarting with dry urine," a smashed instrument, a "stump hanging at the end of the cord" (p. 12).

The vivid clarity that Sammler so directly links to witnessing the activity of the black pickpocket is curiously returned to near the end of the novel while Sammler is conversing with Angela about the antics of her eccentric brother Wallace in the hospital where she and her uncle are awaiting the death of Elya, Angela's father and Sammler's nephew and benefactor. Confronted with Angela's exasperation over the behavior of her brother, her father's lawyer, his doctor, her estranged lover, even to some extent that of her dying father, and, indeed, that of Sammler himself, who is said to be "far from normal" (remembering his recent last view of the pickpocket, his head smashed and blood flowing), Sammler is said somehow to see "everything with heightened clarity." There the tie between the black pickpocket and regained vividness is again made explicit: "As he had seen Riverside Drive, wickedly illuminated, after watching the purse being picked on the bus. That was how he was seeing now" (p. 298). Moreover, what it is that he sees with such clarity is again ambivalently weighed: "To see was delicious. . . . An extreme pleasure!" But "brightness like this, the vividness of everything, also dismayed him" (p. 298). "A barrage of sweetness," to be sure, but also "intolerable brightness. Sammler did not really want to experience this. It all rose against him, too dizzy, too turbulent" (p. 298). The three sparse episodes between Sammler and the thief become for Sammler (and perhaps for us) radiatingly significant; suffice it to say at this point only that they culminate in a Sammler-induced act of vicious violence.

In Bernard Malamud's *The Tenants*, which appeared the next year, 1971, the black/white relationship is avowedly much more center stage, much less episodic, than that in *Mr. Sammler's Planet*. The literal frame in this instance is an abandoned New York tenement wherein, at the novel's opening, Harry Lesser is a solitary occupant trying to finish a novel on which he has been working for ten years. Black writer Willie Spearmint moves uninvited into the flat below Harry's to write on *his* book. The more significant frame, of course, is their mutual occupation. The outside ties—Levenspiel, the landlord who wants to get rid of both so he can demolish the tenement for a more profitable replacement, and Irene Bell, Willie's white Jewish girl who leaves him for Harry—are comparatively insignificant, although Irene is plotted, at least on one level, as the complicating agent. The true complication, however, is white and black—or perhaps, more accurately, Jew and black—although even this conflict is to some extent subsumed under an even broader conflict, that between two views of narrative art. At any rate the conflict between the two is deadly. They mutually destruct. "They aimed at each other accurate blows. Lesser felt his jagged ax sink through the bone and brain as the groaning

black's razor-sharp saber, in a single boiling stabbing slash,
cut the white's balls from the rest of him" (p. 230).[2]

Only in John Updike's *Rabbit Redux*, also published in
1971, is the black/white relationship seen as ending in a
kind of mutual forbearance. Following the burning of his
house and the death of Jill, which Skeeter's presence had
provoked, Harry "Rabbit" Angstrom helps the black Skeeter
flee the law by giving him a car ride to the edge of town and
all the money he has on him. When Harry holds out his hand
to shake farewell, Skeeter cups his hands beneath Harry's,
turns his palm upward, and "solemnly spits into the center"
(p. 336).[3] Harry chooses "to take the gesture as a blessing,
and wipes his palm dry on his pants." As Harry drives off
leaving Skeeter standing there, his final picture of the black,
as reflected in his rearview mirror, looks "oddly right, blends
right in, even with the glasses and goatee, hanging empty-
handed between fields of stubble where crows settle and shift,
gleaning" (p. 337).

These three novels of the early 1970s are all attempts to
catch some aspects of the turbulent 1960s, the civil unrest,
the moon shots, the drug scene, the hippie movement, the
Viet Nam War, the racial strife. That each chose to center his
work on a conflict between a white male and black male
obviously reflects something central about that relationship
in the 1960s, even as it also reflects a contemporary continuation of that long-recognized practice in American fiction (from
James Fenimore Cooper to William Faulkner, at least) to
center attention on male companions of differing colors.[4]
That the efforts of three contemporary novelists as unalike
as Bellow, Malamud, and Updike would, within a period of a
year (and consequently, one could assume, with no knowledge of what the others were doing), parallel one another in
this particular way is strange indeed. To be sure, the racial
strife of the 1960s invited the subject. But for such differing
literary sensibilities to take up that invitation in the particularized way they did suggests that there was during the late
1960s and early 1970s a more cohesive sense, however widely
dispersed, of what one might term literary racial memory or
literary racial consciousness (at least among these three contemporary white writers) than one might have supposed. To
look at these three sets of black/white pairs in these three

modern novels—granting, of course, their distinctive and equally significant differences—is thus to see one significant extension to an often played American literary theme. And however innovative, varied, perhaps even transformed these modern extensions are, it is important to keep in mind their always constrictive similarities.

The Black Pickpocket

The distinctive, innovative mark of Bellow's black is his silence. He never utters a word. The consequent reiterated attention to the details of his appearance—the puma-colored camel's hair coat, the rich cherry-silk necktie, the matching red belt, the single gold earring—give impetus to the visual sense, reinforces the concept of vivid clarity that Sammler associates with the activity of the thief, and of course contributes mightily to the controlled effect of the great mute confrontation when the black quietly displays his penis to Sammler. That astounding scene ultimately keys the novel's racial theme, threads its disparate parts into a cohesive whole, and leads to the novel's resolution, even as it also establishes its central conflict. It deserves close attention.

The scene is prefaced by Sammler's humiliating guest lecture at Columbia University where he is hooted from the stage by a young bearded radical who is described as outraged with an audience listening to what he loudly describes as "this effete old shit" (p. 42). Led from the hall, Sammler boards the Riverside Drive bus to return to his apartment and suddenly finds himself again witnessing the pickpocket in action. This time, however, the black is not quietly, unobtrusively pilfering purses. He is instead openly rifling the wallet of a frightened old man who is sitting alone on the back seat of the bus, shielded from the rest of its occupants by the black's huge back. Only Sammler with his height can see what is going on. A frightened, horrified Sammler makes a quick exit, but not before he sees that the black had seen him. "Seen seeing" Bellow somewhat cutely puts it (p. 47). Sammler dashes into the lobby of the first building he comes to, hoping to elude the thief, hides briefly in a quick-food restaurant with a cup of tea to quiet his palpitating heart, and finally reaches the lobby of his own flat. The black is of course awaiting him there.

Nothing else in the novel quite provokes the reader and, indeed, Sammler himself *and* the other characters who are later told of it in such a variety of significant ways as the great inspired scene that follows. Sammler is silently forced, black belly to white back, into a corner of the lobby:

> There the man held Sammler against the wall with his forearm. . . . The pickpocket unbuttoned himself. Sammler heard the zipper descend. The smoked glasses were removed from Sammler's face and dropped on the table. He was directed, silently, to look downward. The black man had opened his fly and taken out his penis. It was displayed to Sammler with great oval testicles, a large tan-and-purple uncircumcised thing—a tube, a snake; metallic hairs bristled at the thick base and the tip curled beyond the supporting, demonstrating hand, suggesting the fleshy mobility of an elephant's trunk, though the skin was somewhat iridescent rather than thick or rough. Over the forearms and fist that held him Sammler was required to gaze at this organ. No compulsion would have been necessary. He would in any case have looked. [p. 49]

Equally inspired is Bellow's handling of the immediate impact of this act, its effect, its mode:

> The interval was long. The man's expression was not deeply menacing but oddly, serenely masterful. The thing was shown with mystifying certitude. Lordliness. Then it was returned to the trousers. *Quod erat demonstrandum.* Sammler was released. The fly was closed, the coat buttoned, the marvelous streaming silk salmon necktie smoothed with a powerful hand on the powerful chest. The black eyes with a light of super candor moved softly, concluding the session, the lesson, the warning, the encounter, the transmission. He picked up Sammler's dark glasses and returned them to his nose. He then unfolded and mounted his own, circular, of gentian violet gently banded with the lovely Dior gold.
> Then he departed. [pp. 49–50]

The key words describing the black's manner are electrifying: "not deeply menacing but oddly, serenely masterful . . . mystifying certitude. Lordliness . . . *Quod erat demonstrandum*." The variety of nouns that are provided to encapsulate what it is that Sammler has experienced, is equally broad: "the session, the lesson, the warning, the encounter, the transmission." It is, perhaps, the last of these, "the transmission," that is most suggestive.

But before following that possible lead, it should be instructive to look at the variety of ways this confrontation is interpreted by Sammler and others throughout the novel. Sammler's own first interpretation is one of the most provocative—provocative in part because Sammler himself appears only to half-accept his own hypothesis. "What had *that*," he asks, "been about?" "It had given a shock. [And] shocks stimulated consciousness" (p. 55). After dismissing from his mind an unsummoned memory of a classic French anecdote, he goes on in his speculation to describe to himself "the man's organ" as "a prominent and separate object intended to communicate authority, . . . a symbol of superlegitimacy or sovereignty, . . . a mystery . . . ," he continues, "unanswerable. The whole explanation, . . . the wherefore, the why. . . . Oh, the transcending, ultimate, and silencing proof, . . . self-evident" (p. 55). Yet, he can't help continuing, "such elongations the anteater had, too [and] uncomplicated by assertions of power, even over ants." But "elevate creatureliness," he pontificates, "make Nature your God," and "you can count on gross results" (p. 55). Hence, Sammler's first speculation about the black's exhibitory act is a confounding one: a sense of having witnessed primal, self-evident, self-contained thing-in-itself authority, on the one hand; the simultaneous conviction, on the other, that elevating such natural phenomena to divine status inevitably coarsens.

Sammler's next speculation about the black pickpocket follows a comical interruption by a remote relative Walter Bruch, whose peculiar deviation it is to ejaculate in his pants at the sight of dark, plump, round female arms. Sammler no longer tries to put the matter from his mind, but revisualizes the black's penis and describes it to himself as that which strongly suggests "the infant it was there to beget. Ugly, odious; laughable, but nevertheless important" (p. 65). Then he finds himself asserting the variety of ways his and the black's "spiritual profiles were miles apart" (p. 66). Yet, Sammler goes on, he had always thought himself "comely enough, in his own Jewish way," as regards *his* private parts, and had he not once heard that the president of the United States had displayed *his* to the male press, to demonstrate his fitness to lead the country? And was not even "old Picasso's" latest exhibition, to cite still another instance of the "sexual madness [that] was overwhelming the Western world," literally an exhibition of phalluses, "thousands, perhaps tens of thousands" of them? At this troubled thought, Sammler suddenly and unaccountably remembers how his niece Angela had once described "a Jew brain, a black cock, a Nordic beauty" as "what a woman wants" as "the ideal man" (pp. 66–67). Sammler is so depressed by where his own line of reasoning has thus taken him that he becomes "pleasantly haunted by moon-visions," for conditions so austere, so technological, that there would be no time for such troubled behavior.

The final allusion to the black pickpocket in this second chapter joins the thief and Sammler's reaction to him with Sammler's reluctantly acknowledged reaction to Angela's confessions to him of the more sordid details of her freewheeling life-style. He is led to this admission first through the inescapable parallels between the black and Angela's health-food-eating boyfriend Wharton Horricker, in his personal fastidiousness and the sartorial splendor of his custom-made clothes. "The masculine elegance" of the two together is said to constitute "something important, still nebulous, about Solomon in all his glory versus the lilies of the field" that "must be thought about." Angela's contribution to the role played by Horricker leads Sammler to some consideration of the role that he (Sammler) plays with her, as recipient of her various confidences. The unpleasantness of this admission he then faces squarely: "If he heard things he didn't want to hear [from Angela], there was a parallel—on the bus he had seen things he didn't want to see. But hadn't he gone a dozen times to Columbus Circle to look for the black thief?" (p. 69).

Knowledge of the details of the black's exhibition of himself to Sammler is restricted to two other characters, Lionel Feffer, the young opportunistic Columbia professor who arranged Sammler's disastrous lecture there, and his young friend Wallace, Angela's eccentric brother. They react to the act in quite different, although mutually comic, ways. Feffer is fascinated, almost ecstatic, with this example of what he considers modern metropolitan behavior, expresses his intention to get on the bus with a miniature camera to snap the black's picture, talks about selling such a picture to *Look* and getting the black's story on TV, and fantasizes about its possible effect on the political campaign of John Lindsay. Wallace, who learned the details from Feffer, queries Sammler about the color, weight, and length of the black's penis, wonders, in fact, whether Sammler, with his one blind eye, could actually see it, and then further wonders whether women in fact prefer "that kind of thing" (p. 185). This serves merely as preamble to a discussion of women in general (and his sister Angela in particular), of their comparatively more extreme raunchiness (in contrast to men), of their making of everyone between their legs a mere anyone, of their role, in short, of deluding men of their excessive self-importance. He ends abruptly by asking whether the black had shook his "thing" at Sammler. (He had not, as we know.) Sammler retorts, as he had to Feffer, that the black was simply warning him not to defend the poor man he had robbed, not to tell the police. Wallace then makes the curious observation that he has often thought that a man's penis is "expressive," as if "just about to say something, through those whiskers" (p. 188). Having asserted that "blacks speak another language" (p. 188), he tells how a young white boy, surrounded by a group of black thugs, was unsuccessful in begging for his life simply because they did not understand him. Sammler's most significant response to this is a contrasting account of a remembered scene from *War and Peace*, wherein visual communication, in this case a single, momentary, silent glance between executioner and victim prohibits the killing. He goes on to say that he himself has never witnessed such a communication. It nevertheless is not merely "an arbitrary idea. It's based on a belief," he concludes, that "there is the same truth in the heart of every human being, or a splash of God's own spirit, and that this is the richest thing we share in common" (p. 189). However, he continues, "I wouldn't count on it" (count on its being true, that is [p. 189]). This reiterated theory of "silence" is of course tied in with the black's muteness and with Sammler's soundless encounter with him—as an example of an "it" he has indeed witnessed, his protest to the contrary notwithstanding.

Interspersed between and after these two extended comments by characters other than Sammler about the black and his displayed penis is a variety of brief references to the thief, all expressed as if in the consciousness of Sammler and collectively representing various links of meaning still occurring to Sammler about what the black could be said to mean. The first of these is an equation Sammler makes between the thefts by the pickpocket and that by his daughter Shula, who has stolen a manuscript about moon explorations that she wants her father to read. "Suddenly she too was like the Negro pickpocket" (p. 162).[5] More important, perhaps, is the curious generalization Sammler is apparently led to make by this possible parallel: "From the black side," he says, "strong currents were sweeping over everyone. Child, black, redskin—the unspoiled Seminole against the horrible White-man. Millions of civilized people wanted oceanic, boundless, primitive, neckfree nobility, experienced a strange release of galloping impulses, and acquired the peculiar aim of sexual niggerhood for everyone" (p. 162). This first appears to be a rather strong charge against the blacks, but as Sammler meanders on, it becomes clearer that what he sees expressed thereby, via the black, via his daughter, and, reluctantly, via even himself, was only one "experiencing the Age" (p. 162). Later, while discussing Schopenhauer's *World as Will and Idea* with Govinda Lal, the author of the stolen manuscript about possible moon settlements, Sammler explains how the Will, for the German philosopher, is the force, the power, that "drives all things," impervious to everything except ideas, and how we see nothing of this "inner creative fury" except its manifestations. "Like Hindu philosophy," he continues, "Maya, the veil of appearances that hangs over all human experience" (p. 209). He then suddenly remembers that for Schopenhauer the seat of the Will in human beings is "the organs of sex." The black, of course, immediately comes to mind: "The thief in the lobby agreed. He took out the instrument of the Will. He drew aside not the veil of Maya itself but one of its forehangings and showed Sammler his metaphysical warrant" (pp. 209–10).

Among still other brief discursive allusions of this sort, one could mention a final literary tie Sammler makes with the black. Sammler has returned to his Riverside Drive apart-

ment to change shoes and pick up some papers on his way to
visit the dying Elya. Passing out through the lobby he suddenly remembers that it is less than two days since he was
forced "belly-to-back" into a corner by the black. "Unbutton-
ing his puma-colored coat in puma silence to show himself,"
was he, Sammler here asks, "the sort of fellow called by Goethe *eine Nature*? A primary force?" (pp. 281–82). *The* modern
age, contemporary, lawless? A silent but nonetheless all too
visible manifestation of Schopenhauer's Will? Of Goethe's
concept of *eine Nature*? Is the black pickpocket somehow all
of these? Well, yes—and no.

However, the last climactic scene between Sammler and
the black most clearly crystalizes the thief's significance—as
outlaw, as modern, as victim, and indeed, as black, although
the identification that is finally discovered by Sammler is a
sobering identification of himself. That incredible scene happens on Broadway in front of a stopped bus where the black
pickpocket, having seen Feffer snap his picture, has Feffer by
the throat, pushed up against the front of the bus, and is
attempting to take the Minox. Passing on his hurried way to
the dying Elya's bedside, Sammler's car is stopped by his
driver Emil, who recognizes Feffer and directs Sammler to
the action. Sammler immediately guesses what has happened, sees what *is* happening, and is horrified—at Feffer, at
what he has done, at what is being done to him, at the curious
but passive crowd that is gathering, and, in some ways most
of all, at the sight, among the crowd, of a seemingly indifferent, smiling Eisen, his estranged son-in-law, who speaks no
English and who has arrived from Israel only two days before. Unable at first to persuade Eisen to stop the fight, or
Feffer to release the camera, or the black to desist, or, indeed,
anyone in the crowd to interfere, Sammler becomes a sort of
stranger to himself, "a *past* person," somehow, in his solitary
powerlessness, "poor in spirit. Someone between the human
and not-human states, between content and emptiness, between full and void, meaning and not-meaning, between this
world and no world. Flying, freed from gravitation, light with
release and dread, doubting his destination, fearing there
was nothing to receive him" (pp. 289–90).

Just prior to this description of Sammler's state of being,
he is said to study the faces of the on-looking crowd and see
in their interaction a strange quality of expectant gratifica-

tion, "of teased, cheated, famished needs," that "someone was going to get it!" (p. 289). A significant aside at this point, the only racial distinction made during this scene, has Sammler in his mind both divide and rejoin the blacks and whites among the crowd in his awareness that who it was who was "to get it" for the black and whites was different, "another side. But [nevertheless] the same" (p. 289). All, he goes on, were unified by a "beatitude of presence . . . here and not here . . . present while absent . . . [thus] waiting in that ecstatic state" (p. 289).

Their present absence, their state of beatitude, is meant of course as contrast to the absent presence of Sammler, that "*past* person . . . [who] was not himself." All of which leads Sammler now to *command* Eisen to stop the fight. Eisen does so with brutal, devastating, almost fatal efficiency, pounding the black's face with two mighty blows of a baize bag of heavy metal medallions that he was carrying.[6] Hearing the police approaching, they depart, leaving the bloodied Negro on the street. When Emil casually asks who "that black character was," Sammler replies, "I can't really say." As they drive away, Sammler muses to himself: "The black man was a megalomaniac. But there was a certain—a certain princeliness. . . . He was probably a mad spirit. But mad with an idea of *noblesse*. And how much Sammler sympathized with him—how much he would have done to prevent such atrocious blows! How red the blood was, and how thick—and how terrible those crusted, spiny lumps of metal were!" (p. 294).

It is not until sometime later, when Sammler is talking with Angela at the hospital, that he makes the ultimate connection, the connection between violence he has had visited upon the black by Eisen and that that had been visited upon him years before by the Nazis. The parallel is made explicit: "The smash of Eisen's medallions on the pickpocket's face was still with Sammler. His own nerves, in the elementary ways of nerves, connected this with the crushing of his eye under the rifle butt thirty years ago. The sensation of choking and falling—one *could* live through that again. If it was worth living through" (p. 296).

Consequently, the horrifying clarity of vision, the terrifying vivid explicitness, with which Sammler is said to "see" at the end of the novel in his final reference to the black pickpocket is thus not too surprisingly "an intolerable brightness" that he "really did not want to experience." The black pickpocket has finally come to be for Sammler in this last horrendous scene some incredibly bizarre manifestation of his own earlier victimized self. Moreover, he, Artur Sammler, has been the victimizer. "I feel responsible, Emil, because I appealed to Eisen, because I wanted so badly to get to Dr. Gruner" (p. 293). To be sure, still later Sammler appears to mitigate his responsibility for the violence done to the black: "I just saw something peculiarly nasty, on my way over. Partly my fault. I feel distressed" (p. 303). But his final, invidious contrast between Elya and himself—"He did all right. I don't come out nearly so well myself" (p. 303)—and his last words that "each man knows" the terms "of his contract [with God? with Life?]. As I know mine. As all know" (p. 313) clearly reaffirm his true insight into himself.

The too tidy systematizing of relationships at the end of the novel—those of Angela to Elya and to Sammler, of Shula to Sammler, of Sammler to Elya—might from some perspectives appear to be an unwarranted shift of focus from the otherwise more centrally and consistently developed attention to Sammler and the black. But the black who was at first so *exotic* a manifestation, as though from another world, another planet, had finally exposed himself as being all too much a manifestation of Sammler himself, his own planet, and that of those most closely and familiarly around him. Hence, the seemingly adversary relationship between the characters in this first example of modern black/white pairs becomes finally something quite opposite, and perhaps something quite traditional: in America victimized black is still mentor to victimizing white, even to also-victimized Jewish white. Young, crude, powerful Israeli smashes, *at Sammler's instigation*, young princely African thief. That Sammler, in a sense, is both giver and receiver of the near-fatal blow writes an appropriate finis to his former state of near blindness symbolically induced originally by the Nazi rifle butt. The almost unbearable clarity with which he now sees himself and the planet of which he is, inescapably, an inhabitant results most centrally from this irresistible identification with the black pickpocket, his magisterial silence, his princely illegalities, his brutal, near-fatal destruction.

Willie Spearmint

The culminating confrontation between Harry Lesser and Willie Spearmint, the black/white pair in Malamud's *The Tenants*, is much more direct, sensational, and, indeed, final than that in *Mr. Sammler's Planet*. As Harry buries an ax in Willie's skull, remember, the black, with razor-sharp efficiency, simultaneously severs Harry's balls from his body. But even this fatal encounter is also said to be an act of reflexive identification. While in one sense ambivalent, Malamud's one-line postmortem is in another sense explicit: "Each, thought the writer, feels the anguish of the other" (p. 230). The ambivalence, of course, is in the phrase "thought the writer" (Harry, Willie, and/or Malamud?) and in whether the act is "real" or only in Harry's mind. It makes no difference: the asserted cross-identification is unmistakable: "Each . . . feels the anguish of the other."

The pattern in this relationship, unlike that of the black pickpocket and Sammler, begins as a suspiciously adversary one, develops into a sort of companionable collaboration, disintegrates into violent conflict, and concludes with a mutual destructiveness which is nevertheless also clearly another kind of collaboration. Moreover, the race issue is a much more explicit theme here than it is in *Mr. Sammler's Planet*, as are the hierarchies of ties between the two. Both Harry and Willie are dedicated writers; both are in general isolated indifference to the worlds around them; both are in competition for the same girl. Thus racial, aesthetic, cultural, and sexual issues are always, and often too explicitly, the overlaying conflicts.

In the very first scene between the two all of these issues are already incipiently at play. Harry hears the plackity-plak of a typewriter in the building in which he heretofore has been the sole occupant. He discovers that the sound emits from the typing of a black man in the flat next to his, describes the intruder's negroid features and his concentrated indifference to his (Harry's) presence, and wonders what he is doing there (while speculating on how he might be got rid of). Suddenly he is confronted by the black's petulant complaint that he does not like being interrupted: "Can't you see me writing on my book?" "I'm a writer myself," Harry immediately replies (p. 29). In the brief exposition that follows Willie explains how he wandered into the apparently abandoned tenement to find an isolated place to write away from the distractions of his actress girl friend. He expresses his total indifference to whether the "Jew landlord" who owns the building approves of it or not, and, in response to a question, gives the aggressively belligerent information that *what* he is writing "might be fiction but ain't nonetheless real." Harry responds, with some diffidence, that he himself is trying to finish his *third* novel—but then, and almost in spite of himself, he invites Willie to stop by after working hours if he needs anything. In a paragraph of reflection that follows, Harry concludes: "The truth of it is I could do without Willie Spearmint" (p. 33).

The next brief scene between the two begins with Willie stopping by Harry's flat to leave his typewriter. He is impressed with Harry's books and pictures and learns a little more about Harry's background and present occupations. When he discovers a Bessie Smith record, Willie coyly asks, "Are you an expert of black experience?" When Harry replies that he "is an expert of writing," Willie's retort is that he hates "all that shit when whites tell you about black" (p. 36). The scene ends with Willie asking if he can bring some friends up for a party some night soon. Harry is said to be willing—and hopes Willie would "bring along a lady friend or two. He had never slept with a black girl" (p. 37). In the subsequent meeting between the two, after Harry hides Willie from Levenspiel, the landlord, whom Willie describes as a "fartn Jew slumlord," Harry says, "If it's news to you I'm Jewish myself" (p. 41). The white/black confrontation is thus explicitly narrowed to the Jew/black one.[7]

At the party which follows, we learn that Willie's girl is not only white but also (we later learn) Jewish. After Harry unsuccessfully tries to bed Mary Kettlesmith, a black girl who has also come along, Willie and Harry, while stoned, engage in a conversation about their work, art, black, and Jew. Harry describes his book as "about this guy who writes because he has never really told the truth and is dying to" (p. 49). Willie says simply that his is about "Me." They both predict great successes for themselves, which for Harry means immortality and for Willie, money. When Harry brings up the question of art, Willie's impatient reply is, "Don't talk flippy. I worry about it gives me cramps in my motherfuckn liver. Don't say that dirty word" (p. 50). But Harry presses, and Willie then goes into a diatribe about what he calls that "Jewword." The Jews, he continues, are trying to "steal my manhood," wanting to "keep us bloods staying weak so you can take everything for yourself." "Jewgirl" whores, "Jew-doctors," even a "Jewbitch" who once turned a friend of Willie's, he contends, into a fag by persuading him to get circumcised—all are collaborating because "they are afraid if they don't we gon take over the whole goddamn country and wipe you out" (p. 50). "Lesser, you Jewbastard," he concludes, "we tired of you fuckn us over" (p. 51). Harry retorts, "If you're an artist you can't be a nigger, Willie." Willie's last words: "I'm gon drop a atom bomb on the next white prick I see" (p. 51). They nonetheless later depart amicably, embracing "like brothers" (p. 54).

The next episode is probably the most accomplished in the novel—Malamud's account, through Harry, of Willie's book. The day following the party, Willie appears and with great diffidence asks if Harry will read his manuscript. He is eager to do so, but with, of course, some wariness. But his eloquent account of the book's contents, a hundred and forty pages of a black "life" followed by five short stories, is at once the most inventive and in some ways the most compelling episode in the novel. Some of the inspired events said to be in the life and pithy accounts of the central action in each of the stories—especially the one about a black's compulsive "hunger to murder a white and taste a piece of his heart"—may well be one of the best bits Malamud has ever written, simply because it is so beautifully distanced. But Harry's overall response to the manuscript—"an affecting subject" but by one who "has not yet mastered his craft" (p. 66)—is disappointingly predictable, however neat the reflexive revelation that his earlier description about what *his* book was about—"this guy who writes because he has never really told the truth and is dying to" (p. 49)—is, accurately enough, also a description of Willie's.

The painful scene that follows in which Harry informs Willie of his judgment is perhaps also predictable enough, although a marvelous twist is that the part of Willie's book that Harry thought autobiographical is fabricated and the part that seemed fabrication perhaps is not. At any rate,

Willie is outraged, although also obviously hurt, and characteristically resorts to invective. When Harry asserts that "form demands its rights," Willie explodes: "Art can kiss my ass. You want to know what's really art? *I* am art. Willie Spearmint, *black man*. My form is *myself*" (p. 75).[8] But the final sad revelation, after Harry suggests that he get some publishers' opinions, is that Willie's book has already been rejected by ten of what he calls "those rat-brained Jews" (p. 75).

After vanishing for several days, Willie reappears with the surprising news that he has checked Harry's two published novels out of the public library, read them, and come to believe that Harry can teach him something about form. He reiterates that white and black constitute an unbridgeable gap, but he allows that perhaps learning what "whitey" knows and adding on to that what "black" knows will help him out. He announces that he is setting aside for the time being the manuscript that Harry read and is beginning another. He also asks if Harry will help him with some grammar, which Harry agrees to do. Willie has also assumed a new name, Bill Spear.

The next few episodes are marked by a kind of friendly collaboration between the two. Harry helps Willie hide when Levenspiel discovers that the black is in the building and buys him a new table, chair, cot, and lamp to replace those the landlord wrecks. He shares with the reader parts of the first chapter of Willie's new manuscript which he has been asked to read and which he appears to like. They eat and drink together and share thoughts about the art of writing.

Harry's writing, however, is not going well. When he runs into Willie's girl Irene in the Museum of Modern Art one day, we are not surprised to find Harry falling in love with her. But he does not admit it even to himself until some nights later when, at a party of blacks, Willie saves his hide by humiliating him verbally and thus warding off physical violence by other blacks there after they discover that he has sneaked out briefly to bed Mary. But it is Irene whom he really wants. When he finally makes his approach and they bed together, both guilty about Willie, the hokey element in the book is at its most blatant. Although they agree it should be Irene, it is of course Harry who tells Willie. He does so at the worst possible moment, just after having told him how bad the second chapter of his new manuscript is, news that Willie has taken so badly that he has sworn to give up writing altogether. A violent fight erupts, and it seems likely that Harry would have been killed were it not for the unlikely interruption of Levenspiel. Willie runs, beats up Irene, takes his things, and departs. Irene is crushed with guilt but nevertheless hopeful of a future with Harry. They plan to marry and move away—but not until Harry finishes his book.

The increasingly destructive events that rapidly lead to the novel's apocalyptic end are given in a variety of narrative modes. When Harry returns to his rooms, for example, and discovers them ransacked and destroyed, the smokened ashes of his precious manuscript still smoldering on the floor of his tub, we are given Harry's imagined view of how Willie and two friends must have, item by item, step by step, carried out their vendetta, as though they were three robed marauders violating an islanded sanctuary. This is later to be balanced by an imagined double wedding, again isolated and islanded, between Harry and a pregnant black Mary Kettlesmith and between Willie and Irene. A rabbi presides. The ceremonies are Jewish. Its last words, from Irene, as they dance a farewell dance, are "You're not so smart" (p. 217). In between, Harry revises his manuscript, with only feigned complaints at having to do so. Levenspiel increases his pressure on Harry to vacate—with increasingly attractive bribes and with tales of mushrooming familial woe. Irene drifts out of the picture (although she was in no meaningful sense ever in it), but not before she extracts from Harry the revelation that his book, like Willie's, is really writing him. Buildings are crashing down around him. Fires are burning across the street.

Willie suddenly returns, and the two begin devouring one another's literary garbage. What Harry mostly "eats" therefrom is Willie's increasingly shrill anti-Semitic diatribes, the last of which, "The First Pogrom in the U.S. of A.," has the following appended notes as the last written words by Willie that we are to see: "It isn't that I hate the Jews. But if I do any, it's not because I invented it myself but I was born in the good old U.S. of A. and there's a lot of that going on that gets under your skin. And it's also from knowing the Jews, which I do. The way to black freedom is against them" (p. 220).

During the last few pages black and white become more

and more one. Harry stands at Willie's door listening to him type. He imagines Willie at *his* door, also listening. Willie's goatee is now matched by one on Harry. They meet—or are imagined to meet—on the stairs one frigid winter night, Willie on the way up, Harry on the way down. Imprecations alternate (or are imagined as having occurred):

> "I forgive you, Willie, for what you did to me."
> "I forgive you for forgivin me."
> "For burning my book—"
> "For stealin my bitch I love—"
> ". . . I treated you like any other man."
> "No Jew can treat me like a man . . ."
> "You think you are the Chosen People. . . . *We* are the Chosen People." . . .
> "For God's sake, Willie, we're writers. Let's talk to one another like men who write."
> "I dig a different drum than you do, Lesser. . . . On account of you I can't write the way I used to any more." [p. 224]

Neither, it seems, can Harry. So his revenge becomes Willie's. Willie's destruction of Harry's writing becomes Harry's destruction of Willie's writing machine. The black's literary garbage is now as empty as the white's. Their last words to one another before their mutually fatal blows are Willie's "Bloodsuckin Jew Niggerhater" and Harry's "Anti-Semitic Ape" (p. 229).

The central issue here for this essay, distorted though it is by the particularized antagonism of black and Jew, is its exemplification of a modern counterpart to a well-established American literary theme. Sammler is also Jewish; his relation to his black, moreover, is in some ways associated finally to his earlier victimization by the Nazis. Harry and Willie are the inventions of a quite different literary sensibility— one that is more central and enclosed, more narrow *and* more inclusive, than Bellow's example. Yet both literary pairs are finally, at least in some ways, more remarkable for their mutual affinities to a broadly American literary past and modern residue than for their record of Jew/black relations during the 1960s in America.

The final effect of *The Tenants* is to collapse into a single entity concepts of form and content—or of paleface and redskin, to use Rahv's ideological and nationalistic tag words—through undeniably reverberating and equally long-lasting concepts of racial conflict in America. Malamud's controlling rubric of Willie and Lesser's steadfast dedication to the art of writing, however, perhaps blurs on the one hand and over-simplifies on the other both the racial and the aesthetic issues. But both issues are clearly intended to coalesce, the esthetic issue with the racial one no less than the intrinsic conflicts of each, form *and* content, white *and* black.

Introduced as suspicious, competitive adversaries, Harry and Willie finally discover their affinities, although their ultimate affinity—"each feels the anguish of the other"—is simultaneously also their most polarized position. The complementary totems, Harry's brain and his inability to love, Willie's cock and his inability to control, contain their flaws even as they contain their strengths. Hence, what in effect is signaled when white ax smashes into black brain and black knife swishes through white cock is nothing less than an act addressed to another that is more meaningfully an act addressed to oneself. Mutual identification at this cataclysmic point is absolute. Black and white, cock and brain, are imaged as inseparably one. The flowing competitiveness of the two up to this point, with its perhaps too schematic expanding corollaries of racial, aesthetic, and sexual conflicts, is fatally, if mercifully, resolved. Yet the conflict itself recapitulates the history of racial and esthetic strife in America, resolving it in mutual self-destruction, one popular "answer" of the 1960s, "apocalypse now." But insofar as it equates the claims of both sides as necessary and legitimated, it simultaneously conceptualizes some ultimately "possible" whole.

For Malamud authentic occupancy in this fictional tenement is only for whites who are also black, or vice versa—form that is also content.

Skeeter

Interestingly enough, the black/white pair in John Updike's *Rabbit Redux*, like that in *The Tenants*, is first significantly thrown together when the black, Skeeter, intrusively moves into the dwelling of the white, Harry Angstrom. Also as in *The Tenants*, there is a complicating white girl, the young hippie, Jill, with ties to the black that predate the developing ones with Rabbit.[9] Like *Mr. Sammler's Planet*, moreover, *Rabbit Redux* counterpoints its black/white action with a context of moon exploration. In this regard, it perhaps should be noted that only a few years earlier, in 1965, Norman Mailer, in *An American Dream*, had written of a black/white pair, the white Steve Rojack and the black Shago Martin, and a complicating white girl who was intimate with both. In that work also images of the moon served as a thematic strategy. Even so, there is another, more intimate context for *Rabbit Redux* that necessarily precedes the more basic concern here with Updike, Bellow, and Malamud. That is *Rabbit, Run*, of which *Rabbit Redux* is the sequel. The rich achievement of Updike's rendition of the black/white pair in this sequel is, to some extent at least, dependent upon its contextual relation to its forerunner.

At the end of that earlier novel, Rabbit is still running. Its last words are "he runs. Ah: runs. Runs." But the Rabbit of *Rabbit Redux* is not running. It is now ten years later. Rabbit has returned to his wife Janice, and he is almost perfectly still, passive, cold, empty, sedentary. Approaching middle age, fattening at the gut, he has turned reactionary through the threat of change. Yet, change is precisely what works so brilliantly in *Rabbit Redux*, and the rendered ways of that change are really impressive. Fine as *Rabbit, Run* is, it is not as fine as *Rabbit Redux*, not as ambitious, not as complex, not as aesthetically rich. The controlling space imagery, to cite a single example, is much more variously deployed than is the basketball imagery of the earlier volume. Yet, that the basketballs *become* moonshots gives a richness to both that neither could quite sustain alone.

Still other continuities are variously established. The first is set in spring and early summer (the time of growth), the other in late summer and early autumn (the time of death). Rabbit's adultery in the first parallels Janice's in the second. Janice has inadvertently drowned their baby daughter; Rabbit assumes some of the responsibility for the burning of Jill. The concept of restless quester among those who wished Rabbit to remain constant (in *Rabbit, Run*) is richer still when expressed as a now-stubborn conservatism among those who urge change (as in *Redux*). "In the early novel," as Robert Detweiler puts it, "for all his struggle to change, he cannot; in the sequel, for all his struggle to remain the same, he changes."[10] In *Run*, inept, childish, ineffective, even destructive dreamer though Rabbit was, he was also the only character with a sense of belief strong enough to vitalize others. But in *Redux* Skeeter's hate becomes the vitalizing agent — and, ironically enough, it is also Skeeter who reveals himself to be the new embodiment of the American Dream, the dreamer *and* the dream (in a way), piquantly replacing the early Rabbit as basketball star as he reveals himself to be the more adept "shooter."

What "happens" in *Rabbit Redux* is surprisingly simple. Harry has returned to his wife Janice, but their life together is cold and stale. She commits adultery with Charlie Stavros, a Greek-American car salesman who works for her father. When Rabbit discovers the affair, he lets her go and takes up with a young, classy hippie, Jill, and a black Viet Nam veteran and pusher, Skeeter, who is on the run from the law. Neighborhood arsonists burn down the Angstrom house, where Skeeter and Jill are staying, and Jill is killed. Skeeter departs, and Rabbit and Janice come warily back together.

The variety of relationships in this deceptively simple plot is astounding — each character touching and being touched by each of the others: Harry to Janice *and* to her lover, to his dying mother and elderly father, to his Las Vegas call-girl sister, Mim (a former Disneyland guide), to his thirteen-year-old son, Nelson, to Jill, and, most important, to Skeeter. It is, finally, his relationship to the black that most affects his relationships with everyone else. The black's vitalizing hate and knowledge and eloquence are the catalytic agents that move Harry out of his somewhat troubled and grumbling passivity. Frame and context for this reluctant transformation are drenched with aspects of American life of the 1960s — Viet Nam War, black revolution, drug addiction, middle-class anger and frustration, hippie life-styles, the moon-shot. But the only public vitality envisioned in this cultural milieux derives from the vitriolic passion of Skeeter (excepting for the moment, the awakened sensuality of Janice as an example of "personal" or private vitality).

What develops between Rabbit and Skeeter between their initial, antagonistic meeting in Jimbo's Friendly Lounge and the "blessing" that Rabbit interprets the black's final act toward him to be is one of the most dramatically charged and poignantly developed accounts of racial confrontation in our literature. Although reflecting all of the standard shibboleths—distrust, suspicion, sexual rivalry (and ambivalent sexual attraction), and various degrees of violence—it is the first example in white American fiction since Faulkner that appears to accept the premise that black America knows white America better than white America knows itself. Skeeter throughout is the acknowledged mentor; Rabbit is the reluctant student at the beginning, but he becomes increasingly eager.

What is first established in the lounge—other than our introduction to the wit and erudition and hate of Skeeter, with his "silver circular glasses and a little pussy of a goatee" (p. 115)—is the symbolic parenthood assumed by the black singer, Babe, and her friend Buchanan who invited Harry to the lounge to explore whether he can be enticed, or persuaded, to take over the care and feeding of the white runaway, Jill, who has been living with Babe. "Mothers and fathers, they turn up everywhere" (p. 128). Babe, elsewhere, says about Jill that she "is my baby-love and I'm her mama-love" (p. 129). Even Harry is said to feel that "he's found another father" (p. 127) in one reference to Buchanan. At one point, in fact, this familial trope is so extended as to include the hate-spewing Skeeter as Harry's "brother," although the occasion for that particular expression of fraternal benevolence is brought on by the dual narcotics of Babe's music and pot (p. 125).

The unlikely notion of Harry and Jill as "children" of this black community has back of it (whatever the echoes of Twain's Jim in *Huckleberry Finn* or Faulkner's Dilsey in *The Sound and the Fury*) the even more unlikely notion that the only residue left of the American Dream is somehow now in the voices of the blacks. Listening to the songs Babe plays, Harry recognizes

> lyrics born in some distant smoke, decades when
> America moved within the American dream, laughing
> at it, starving on it, but living it, humming it, the
> national anthem everywhere. Wise guys and hicks,
> straw boaters and bib overalls, fast bucks, broken hearts,

penthouses in the sky, shacks by the railroad tracks, ups
and downs, rich and poor, trolley cars, and the latest
news by radio. Rabbit had come in on the end of it, as the
world shrank like an apple going bad and America was
no longer the wisest hick town within a boat ride of
Europe, and Broadway forgot the tune, but *here it all
still was*, in the music played. [p. 124; emphasis added]

The rich irony in Harry's reading of black music in this
nostalgic way—he is, after all, the only white in this black
bar—is double-edged in its implications. His total ignorance
of black America and of black interpretations of its dream is
obvious in his attribution of his own white sentimentality to
these black lyrics. But more important is the reversed residue of the dream within the blacks. At the baseball game
attended by Rabbit, his son Nelson, and his father-in-law
Springer, the game, "whose very taste, of spit and dust and
grass and sweat and leather and sun, was America" (p. 85),
could no longer enchant; its "code" was no longer capable of
yielding its meaning. Its single residual vitality was in racial
hate; the crowd's single spark of "life" was witnessing white
pitcher against black batter: "Ram it down his throat,
Speedy!" "Kill the black bastard!" (p. 83). Hence, more than
surface irony is involved when Skeeter lectures Rabbit on
quintessential manifest destiny, American style, especially
as represented by Viet Nam. Rabbit has asked whether "our
being in Viet Nam" is "wrong":

Wrong? Man, how can it be wrong when that's the way it
is? These poor Benighted States just being themselves,
right? Can't stop bein' Yourself, somebody has to do it for
you, right? Nobody that big around. Uncle Sam wakes
up one morning, looks down at his belly, sees he's some
cockroach, what can he do? Just keep bein' his cockroach
self, is all. Till he gets stepped on. No such shoe right
now, right? Just keep doing his cockroach thing. I'm not
one of these white lib-er-als like that cracker Fulldull or
Charlie McCarthy a while back gave all the college
queers a hard on, think Vietnam some sort of mistake,
we can fix it up once we get the cave men out of office, it
is *no* mistake, right, any President comes along falls in
love with it, it is lib-er-alism's very wang, dingdong
pussy, and fruit. Those crackers been lickin' their moth-

er's ass so long they forgotten what she looks like frontwards. What is lib-er-alism? Bring joy to the world, right? Puttin' enough sugar on dog-eat-dog so it tastes good all over, right? Well now what could be nicer than Vietnam? We is keepin' that coast open. Man, what is we all about if it ain't keepin' things open? How can money and jizz make their way if we don't keep a few cunts like that open? Nam is an act of love, right? Compared to Nam, beatin' Japan was flat-out ugly. We was ugly fuckers then and now we is truly civilized spot. . . . We is *the* spot. Few old fools like the late Ho may not know it, we is what the world is begging *for*. Big beat, smack, black cock, big-assed cars and billboards, we is into *it*. Jesus come down, He come down here. These other countries, just bullshit places, right? We got the *ape* shit, right? Bring down Kingdom Come, we'll swamp the world in red-hot real American blue-green ape shit, right?" [pp. 263–64]

Updike's achievement with the picture of Skeeter is the finest stroke in the novel, the most audacious of Updike's borrowed voices (which had surely been audacious enough in creating Henry Bech as a contemporary Jewish novelist, not to mention that of the much more recent Colonel Hakim Félix Elleloû in *The Coup*). Skeeter is the character with whom Updike risks the most—but also the one through whom he gains the most. His successful realization was extremely improbable. Detweiler's list highlights the improbabilities: "Vietnam War veteran turned anti-war, drug dealer, self-proclaimed revolutionary, and black messiah" but also "traumatized war veteran, minor criminal, seducer and lover, racial avenger and redeemer. He lives his paranoia in fear of white persecution and in the delusion of grandeur as self-styled savior"[11]—true-blue, black/white quintessential American, in short. He works, moreover, both as messiah, however ironically, *and* as culpably human (his part in allowing Jill's death). Indeed, he works, in one way or another, in each of the roles in this list and, finally, in the most believable black language of any writer, black or white, writing in the last two decades in America.[12]

No less improbably and yet somehow dramatically right is the relation of Rabbit to this curiously conceived black. When

Skeeter first moves in, for example, his exasperating tactic—to goad Rabbit into attacking him physically and then, through guilt for having done so, allowing him to stay—is a perfectly conceived reading of Rabbit's character. After first taunting Rabbit with vulgar blasphemy about a "white" Christ, he bumps Harry with this brilliantly parodic expletive: " 'Hey. Wanna know how I know? Wanna know? Hey, I'm the real Jesus. I am *the* black Jesus, right? There is none other, no. When I fart, lightning flashes, right? Angels scoop it up in shovels of zillion-carat gold. Right? Kneel down, Chuck. Worship me. I am Jesus. Kiss my balls, they are the sun and the moon, right, and my pecker's a comet whose head is the white-hot heart of the glory that never does fail.' And, his head rolling like a puppet's, Skeeter unzips his fly and prepares to display this wonder" (p. 210).

The "school" he later sets up for Rabbit's edification begins with equal improbability; yet, it too is somehow dramatically right. As Rabbit thumbs through Skeeter's pathetic little library, for example (*The Selected Writings of W. E. B. Du Bois, The Wretched of the Earth, Soul on Ice, The Life and Times of Frederick Douglass*), Skeeter shouts out: "Hey Chuck . . . know where I got those books? Over in Nam, the Longbinh base bookstore. They love us to read, that crazy Army of yours. Teach us how to read, shoot, dig pot, sniff scag, black man's best friend, just like they say" (p. 226). His introductory lesson, "a kind of seminar, about Afro-American history" (p. 229), as Jill puts it, not Skeeter's "personal history so much as the history of his race, how he got here" (p. 229), is eloquently given. In a moving and believable scene the opening "subject," the sellout of blacks during the post–Civil War period through the collusion of Northern industrialists and Southern planters, brings Skeeter to tears.

When his final "point" about how the white sellout of the black was more tellingly a white sellout of self—"you really had it here, you had it all, and you took that greedy mucky road, man, you made yourself the asshole of the planet" (p. 234)—moves Rabbit to an at least mild protest—"Trouble with your line . . . it's pure self pity" (p. 234)—Skeeter shrewdly counters with still another perpetual element in black/white relations in America: the white attraction to and fear of the black: "We fascinate you, white man. We are in your dreams. We are technology's nightmare. We are all the good satisfied nature you put down in yourselves when you took that mucky greedy turn. We are what has been left *out* of the industrial revolution, so we are the *next* revolution, and don't you know it? You know it. Why else you so scared of me, Rabbit?" Rabbit can reply to this particular barb only with the weak, punning "Because you're a spook" (p. 235).

Skeeter's subsequent "lectures" on the black experience, slavery, the coming revolution, class struggle, and sex are equally telling. But perhaps nowhere in this relationship does Updike risk quite so much as he does in presenting Rabbit's barely contained attraction to Skeeter's blackness. A skin-thin texture of eroticism was never totally absent from either Bellow's or Malamud's black/white pair. But in neither of these examples did it surface with quite the explicit daring displayed by Updike. Relatively early in the Skeeter chapter we are told that "physically, Skeeter fascinates Rabbit." Updike then continues: "The lustrous pallor of the tongue and palms and the soles of the feet, left out of the sun. Or a different kind of skin? White palms never tan either. The peculiar glinting lustre of his skin. The something so very finely turned and finished in the face, reflecting light at a dozen polished points: in comparison white faces are blobs: putty still drying. The curious greased grace of his gestures, rapid and watchful as a lizard's motion, free of mammalian fat. Skeeter in his house feels like a finely made electric toy; Harry wants to touch him but is afraid he will get a shock" (p. 251).

In the climactic scene of his weird menage, Updike successfully integrates all of these explosive elements into a cohesive whole. Rabbit, by now smoking one of Skeeter's joints, is reading an eloquent passage from *The Life and Times of Frederick Douglass* wherein the white "master" is brutally and sadistically flogging a black female slave whose love for another slave the "Colonel" has imperiously forbidden. The mixture of sentiment and violence transfixes the whites; *their* fascination with it, no less than the passage itself, drives Skeeter almost delirious. He turns on Jill, rips her dress, strips off his own shirt, and offers the frightened young Nelson his belt, inviting young Babychuck, as Skeeter calls him, to flog him. Nelson flees the room. Rabbit sits transfixed, his eyes glued, we are told, to Skeeter's "skinny chest," which is "stunning in its articulation: every muscle sharp in its attachment to the bone, the whole torso carved in a jungle wood darker than shadow and more dense than ivory. Rabbit has never seen such a chest except on a crucifix" (p. 279). As Rabbit continues with the passage, which first quiets and then reexcites Skeeter until he is literally grappling with Jill on the couch, Rabbit views Jill's smile, "her small gray teeth bare in silent laughter . . . liking it, being raped" (p. 280). Seeing Rabbit see her, Jill, like Nelson, departs. Rabbit and the undressed Skeeter are now left alone. It is at this point that white and black are depicted in an incredibly erotic stance: Skeeter driven to apparently masturbatory ecstasy by Rabbit's eloquent reading from Douglass, is in a kind of syndicated revivalistic bliss—"Yes. . . . Yes. . . . Oh yes. Yes. . . . A-men. . . . Say it. Say it. . . . Oh, you do make one lovely nigger" (pp. 282–83); Rabbit, equally driven apparently by the pitch of ecstasy to which his reading had excited Skeeter, only just escapes the incantatory "pull," that "whispering rhythm that wants to suck him forward" (p. 283). Rabbit flees upstairs—but impotently—to Jill. But even sleep does not come, we are told, until "within himself, Rabbit completes his motion into darkness, into the rhythmic brown of the sofa" (p. 284).

It is a remarkably effective scene, everywhere fraught with hazards and boldly inclusive of such a wide variety of sexual and racial elements that its psychological, sociological, and, indeed, historical overlays surface only upon reflection. Updike, it seems to me, in essaying such a confrontation, risks much more than either Bellow or Malamud. His final resolution between the two—after the burning of the house, the death of Jill, and the consequent disaffection of the young Nelson—somehow comes out all right, through Skeeter's "assisted" flight, the expectorated "blessing," and perhaps even the too obvious semiotic "Galilee 2" that signals the crossroad where Skeeter is left.

"Never did figure your angle," Skeeter tells him, as Rabbit prepares to leave. "Probably wasn't one," Rabbit replies. "Just waiting for the word, right?" (p. 336). Skeeter "cackles" as *his* final word.

"Waiting for the word" is not an inappropriate tag for Rabbit's final relation with the novel's other major characters, his hippie-mistress "daughter" Jill (almost a mixture of James's Maisie Farange and Nabokov's Lolita) no less than

the now wiser, returned wife, Janice. For when, near the end
of the novel, Harry observes to Janice that "all this fuck-
ing . . . makes . . . [him] too sad. It's what makes everything
so hard to run," it is Janice who replies, "You don't think it's
what *makes* things run? Human things?" And when Harry
retorts, "There must be something else" (pp. 398–99), that
"something else" is surely the same ineffable "word" that
Skeeter had so deftly posed as key to Rabbit's need.[13]

Old-fashioned Moderns?

Rabbit Angstrom and Skeeter, Bellow's Mr. Sammler and
the black pickpocket, Malamud's Harry Lesser and Willie
Spearmint, and, on one level, even Mailer's Steve Rojack and
Shago Martin are all reverberating echoes. Plucked from the
peculiar nature of American racial history, refurbished and
embellished to fit the needs of these talents at a particular
time, they nonetheless clearly constitute a *collective* comment.
Two of the critics who have given published attention to this
collective element both think, as I do, that Updike's handling
of the black/white relationship in *Rabbit Redux* is superior
to that of Bellow and Malamud.[14] For Richard Locke, the
blacks in *Mr. Sammler's Planet* and *The Tenants* come "nowhere near the depth and accuracy of Updike's black characters."[15] For Robert Alter, in his much more extended treatment of this issue (although limited in its major thrust to
Rabbit Redux and *The Tenants*), Updike is ultimately more
plausible than Malamud, the "extremeness" of Skeeter and
the irresolution of the ending notwithstanding. He views
Malamud's position as too abstract, parablelike, schematic,
and Lesser's "self-victimization" too much a matter "of individual obsession." On the other hand, "Angstrom's self-
victimization bespeaks a publicly shared feeling of guilt."[16]

     In my own view, Updike's comparatively greater success in
dealing with this issue stems from his more distanced and
perhaps more imaginative concept of character. The Rabbit/
Skeeter relationship, interestingly enough, is conceived in a
manner almost diametrically opposite to the relationships
given by Bellow and Malamud. For Bellow the black pick-

pocket is no more than a mime, a symbol, a totem—brilliantly rendered, to be sure, but always there for what he reveals about Sammler (however wide the variety of speculation by Sammler himself and indeed by his white associates about what he *could* mean), not for what he is as a thing-in-himself. Only Sammler is a thinker, an intellectual, a "writer." Although Malamud's Lesser and Willie are both conceived as unfulfilled writers possessed to a fault by each other's lack, it is Lesser who is rendered as ultimately having "more" (his name to the contrary notwithstanding)—if only by virtue of finally being pictured as one who both thinks and feels in contrast to the merely "feeling" Willie, as John Murray Cuddihy so perceptively pointed out soon after the novel appeared.[17] But in Updike, Skeeter is the contrasting intellectual-historian-teacher (among his many other roles). It is thus by a black thinker that the white Rabbit Angstrom is so fearfully, reluctantly, and yet at least half-successfully schooled. Although Skeeter is more exaggerated, more extreme, than either the black pickpocket or Willie Spearmint (as Alter contends), only Skeeter is also sufficiently strong to survive as a character who is not also merely a symbol, an idea.

Finally, Updike also dares a great deal more than the other two in the explicit eroticism he conceives as part of Rabbit's love/hate relationship with Skeeter, a concept of reflexive identification between his white and black ("Oh, you do make one lovely nigger," Skeeter "sings" at Rabbit) that is much more natural and less schematic than the highly symbolic and somewhat pretentious cross-identifications made by the other two. Alter is surely right when he concludes that, although "deeply shaken" and "figuratively burned" by his extended encounter with Skeeter, Rabbit nonetheless "plausibly remains more or less what he was," however "now shot through with doubts about what America has really been" and however "more clearly" he now sees blacks as human beings and "understands in some way the exigencies of their troubled condition." The vague but undeniable sense of complicity that Rabbit is depicted as possessed by at the end of the novel is indeed an uneasy resolution. But the disequilibrium itself is what finally works so beautifully, and Alter's conclusion that the novel as a whole "says something that sounds right about where we are now"[18] is not to be gainsaid.

Even so, where we are now, I would conclude, is in fact

somewhere near the literary position white American novelists have maintained for a long time: black victim to white victimizer becomes black mentor to white pupil; the self-revelatory nature of the victimization is itself a catalyst toward some new knowledge of self that leads to some new knowledge of another, or vice versa. Some such simple rubric would not be, on one level, an inappropriate gloss to the Huck/Jim relationship in *Huckleberry Finn*. Although in much more devious and complex ways, it might be said to apply as well to works as distant and different from Twain's as Melville's earlier *Benito Cereno* or any number of Faulkner's quite later works (*Go Down, Moses*, for example, or *Intruder in the Dust*). Among these recent examples, Artur Sammler's enlarged, corrected, and finally vivid "vision" is said to have resulted directly from his complicity in the mauling of the black pickpocket. Harry Lesser's white blow at Willie's black brain, whether real or imagined, is some kind of anguished blow at a new, more collaborative self. Finally, it is clearly Rabbit Angstrom's extended and complex confrontations with Skeeter that more tellingly than anything else bring him back to a kind of health from the lethargic apathy under which he suffers when the novel opens.

This shared element notwithstanding, *Mr. Sammler's Planet*, *The Tenants*, and *Rabbit Redux* are, of course, radically different novels, the products of quite disparate literary sensibilities, and each is perhaps ultimately more meaningful in the context of each author's canon than in any other. Yet, this tie—through their adaptations of a common literary past that perhaps all too abruptly became a compulsively common literary present—also has its own significance. The black/white relation in contemporary America—at least as given us through the talented imaginations of these three contemporary novelists—finally reveals itself to be an old, old story, however new the collective urgency to reconfront it and however varied the styles, voices, and tactics employed.

SIX

Three Applications

THE THREE BRIEF essays that follow are extensive and varied applications of the informal methodology governing the previous chapters, with a radical change in the concept of context. Although each essay remains a discrete critical entity, an overall concept of context continues to determine each reading. The common context, for example, for the digressions in Melville's *Billy Budd* is internally reflexive "readings" of the tale itself. In the essay on the James story "The Birthplace" the context is the place of a work of literary art in the plethora of critical attention its author has engendered. In the last of the pieces, a consideration of three early novels by Faulkner, the context is the literary environment in which a particular body of creative work flourished. The readings that result from these various contexts are, of course, as different as the contexts themselves. At the same time it is the contextual "glow" that determines what each reading is.

Truth's Ragged Edges: Melville's Loyalties in *Billy Budd*— The Commitment of Form in the Digressions

The adaptations of Melville's *Billy Budd* by librettists, playwrights, scenarists, and other borrowers is of less concern to me in this essay than the adaptations by Melville himself of comparable forms (mostly in the popular oral arts) within the tale. The perfectly rendered final image of the hanging scene, the place in the tale where all the outside adaptations end, is of less interest to me here than those so-called digressions that follow it—digressions that Melville deliberately included, I contend, in order at least to ruffle the implications of a tale without them. But the hanging scene is great—because it is so charged, yet so balanced; so tense, yet so (seemingly) resolved.

The bare events preceding the hanging are straightforward and simple enough. A young British sailor is impressed into service on a man-of-war, the *Bellipotent*, from a merchant ship named the *Rights of Man*. Artless, guileless, outgoing, and friendly, he immediately wins the friendship of all the men on board with the exception of John Claggart, the ship's master of arms, who, for a variety of reasons, finds Billy's presence on board anathema and plots to destroy him. He finally contrives to summon Billy before Captain Vere, the commander of the vessel, and there falsely accuses him of mutiny. In his anger at the charge and because of his inability to speak—he stutters when nervous—Billy strikes Claggart, who falls dead at his feet. Captain Vere, although very fond of Billy, whom he knows to be innocent, nonetheless orders a court martial on the charge of having struck a superior during a time of war. Discovering the other officers of the ship reluctant to find Billy guilty, Vere forces a verdict and sentences Billy to death by hanging. Following an undisclosed colloquy between the captain and Billy the night before, the verdict is carried out. However, Billy publicly blesses the captain the moment before he is hanged.

Billy utters his benediction on the man responsible for his hanging, "God Bless Captain Vere,"[1] in "syllables unanticipated coming from one with the ignominious hemp about his neck . . . [and] delivered in the clear melody of a singing bird on the point of launching from the twig." The effect of this utterance, we are told, was "phenomenal," and the ship's populace is described as reacting to it in concert as if they were "but vehicles of some vocal current electric."

Vere's reaction at this precise point is quite different. For "at the pronounced words and the spontaneous echo that voluminously rebounded them . . . either through stoic self-control or a sort of momentary paralysis induced by emotional shock, [he] stood erectly rigid as a musket in the ship-armorer's rack." The scene's penultimate paragraph is then rendered as follows: "The hull, deliberately recovering from the periodic roll to leeward, was just regaining an even keel when the last signal, a preconcerted dumb one, was given. At the same moment it chanced that the vapory fleece hanging low in the East was shot through with a soft glory as of the fleece of the Lamb of God seen in mystical vision, and simultaneously therewith, watched by the wedged mass of upturned faces, Billy ascended; and, ascending, took the full rose of the dawn" (p. 68). Melville concludes this scene with a magisterial sentence: "In the pinioned figure arrived at the yard-end, to the wonder of all no motion was apparent, none save that created by the slow roll of the hull in moderate weather, so majestic in a great ship ponderously cannoned" (p. 69).

The aesthetic balance here must be readily apparent: the association of Billy with "melody," flight, softness, "mystical vision"; that of Vere with silence, stillness, rigidity, stasis. The poetic, rhetorical, imagistic coup in the passage, however, is in the final portion, where the opposing forces are joined (and transformed), made literally and symbolically interdependent, aesthetically, in short, *resolved*; for the majestic sweep of the great "slow roll of the hull" is precisely and restrictively defined as possible only with "a great ship ponderously cannoned."

Hence, the mountain of criticism given over during the more than fifty years since the tale was discovered in the early 1920s to the question of whether *Billy Budd* is pro-Vere or anti-Vere, a testament of acceptance or of rebellion, humanistic or nihilistic, straightforward or ironic, is, on this stylistic level, simply beside the point. Billy and Vere have no meaning except as they relate to one another; Melville's loyalties can certainly not be said to be given to one any more than to the other. What can be said is that every resource of language that Melville had at his command is here beautifully brought into play to render a memorable, transcendent moment of majestic movement through the imagistic and symbolic joining of richly suggestive opposites: The now *motionless* pinioned figure at one with the slow roll of the great ship ponderously cannoned, rhythm and syntax as irrevocably committed to the joining as imagery and symbol.

It is of course a crucial aspect of the tale and precisely the point at which the many eminent adaptations end, including the dramatic version by Louis O. Coxe and Robert Chapman, the operatic one by Benjamin Britten and its libretto by E. M. Forster, and, for all practical purposes, the widely viewed cinematic and television version adapted, directed, and starred in by Peter Ustinov.

Melville's story, however, continues, and the five chapters that follow the hanging scene are no less a part of the tale than the hanging scene itself. Although these chapters have been looked at often enough for a variety of specialized reasons—as a sort of coda to tidy up the aftermath of the hanging, as a repository of an excerpted detail to support one or another particular interpretation of the tale proper, or, in Robert Penn Warren's case, as attention to a single digression, the ballad, as part of his overall interest in Melville's poetry—very rarely have they been considered as important as the material preceding and including the benediction and hanging.[2] The single exception of which I am aware is a short paper by Mary Foley, a former student of mine, who wrote the paper under my direction and which appears in my edition of *Billy Budd and the Critics* (1963, pp. 220–23). Even it, however, is much more narrowly focused than these remarks.

The first digression, chapter 26, is a marvelously humorous conversation between the ship's surgeon and its purser on the subject of why there was no muscular spasm, no erected penis, at the moment of hanging, as we are given to believe is normal in such cases. They speculate that Billy willed his death and stopped his heart before the hanging, perhaps, they say, as a form of euthanasia. But this they both dismiss as unscientific and agree only that it was phenomenal, having causes, "the cause of which is not immediately to be assigned" (p. 69). The word *euthanasia* is described as at once "imaginative and metaphysical," hence, "not scientific." They change the subject and withdraw.

Chapter 27 is devoted to how, before and following the burial of Billy at sea, the restless, murmuring, muttering crew is kept in line by Vere's disciplined forcing of them to perform trivial, tedious tasks. "Forms, measured forms," Vere says, "are everything" (p. 71). Earlier in this chapter the narrator observes that "true martial discipline long continued superinduces in average man a sort of impulse whose operation at the official word of command much resembles in its promptitude the effect of an instinct" (p. 71).

Chapter 28 begins with the narrator's little joke, the often-quoted statement that "the symmetry of form attainable in pure fiction cannot so readily be achieved in a narration essentially having less to do with fable than with fact. Truth uncompromisingly told will always have its ragged edges," he continues, as if pure fiction would not (p. 72). The tone then abruptly changes with the statement that "how it fared with the Handsome Sailor during the year of the Great Mutiny has been faithfully given. But though properly the story begins with his life, something in way of sequel will not be amiss" (p. 71). Three brief chapters will suffice, he says, as though two had not already been given.

What then follows is the account of the shooting of Captain Vere while attempting to board an enemy ship named the *Athié* (formerly the *St. Louis*). In that battle the *Bellipotent* was nonetheless finally victorious. Afterward, Captain Vere was landed at Gibraltar, where he died with the words "Billy Budd, Billy Budd" on his lips—words, we are told, that "were inexplicable to his attendant" (p. 72). "That these were not the accents of remorse *would seem* clear from what the attendant said to the *Bellipotent*'s senior officer of marines" (p. 72, emphasis added).

Chapter 29 is an ironic newspaper account, from a naval chronicle of the time, under the heading "News from the Mediterranean." In it we are told how John Claggart was "vindictively stabbed to the heart" by one William Budd, whom Claggart had been arraigning before the captain as ringleader of a plot; how Budd was surely not his true name and he no Englishman in view of the deed he had committed; and how his victim, John Claggart, "was a middle-aged man respectable and discreet" (p. 73). It goes on to point out how the "criminal paid the penalty of his crime" and how "the promptitude of the punishment has proved salutary. Nothing amiss is now apprehended aboard H.M.S. *Bellipotent*" (p. 73).

The final chapter, chapter 30, is an account of how years later the spar from which Billy was suspended became to some of the crew, "ignorant though they were of the secret facts of the tragedy," as though "a chip of it [were] a piece of the Cross" (p. 74). The last item is the ballad "Billy in the Darbies," which presents a Billy totally unlike the other Billy Budds we have thus far seen: a Billy who is a raconteur, a wit, a man of words cynically capable of describing his own pendant hanging from the yardarm as like the "ear drop" he gave to one Bristol Molly, presumably his port whore. The author of the ballad, we are told, was some foretopman who followed Billy, "gifted, as some sailors are, with an artless *poetic* temperament," here giving "rude utterance" to "the general estimate of [Billy's] nature and its unconscious simplicity" (p. 74).

These, then, are the events Melville so carefully and often so wittingly gives after the event of Billy's hanging: the momentary speculation of the purser and the surgeon about the absence of any muscular spasm in Billy immediately following the hanging; the restlessness of the crew and how they were kept in check by Captain Vere, who pushed them through a variety of petty menial forms; the death of Vere in an encounter with a ship called the *Athié*, the words "Billy Budd, Billy Budd" on his lips; the newspaper account which views Claggart as the epitome of heroic patriotism and Billy as treacherous villain; a report of how some of the sailors viewed the yardarm from which Billy was hanged as though it had been a piece of the cross; and a ballad, said to be written by another foretopman, which depicts Billy as a witty, sophisticated, worldly cynic.

Considering the strategy of these events as rendered, we might first note the chronological order of their arrangement, moving *from* the event to the tale itself: the first two events follow the hanging in relatively rapid succession, followed by a greater and greater extension of time between the succeeding ones—the death of Vere, the newspaper account, the sailors' superstition, the ballad. Melville's account, the tale he gives us, presumably follows that—both "in fact" (note the quotations) and, more important, in the fiction itself. (I say "in fact" because one of the provocative revelations in Hayford and Sealt's genetic text of the tale, their account of how the tale was written, is that Melville began with the ballad and worked backwards. The complex, ambivalent, and perhaps contradictory role of Vere became the last addition to the ultimately unfinished tale.) But even in the fiction itself we see this clearly articulated "game"—in the narrator's comment, for example, after the newspaper account, that "the above [referring to that account] is all that hitherto has stood in human record to attest what manner of men respectively were John Claggart and Billy Budd" (p. 73).

We also have the comment, in chapter 28, the third digression, that "how it fared with the Handsome Sailor during the year of the Great Mutiny has been faithfully given" (p. 72). In a sense, then, we see an increasing distortion of the Billy of the tale proper—the Billy of the ballad is less like the Billy of the tale than is the Billy of the newspaper chronicle. Such a conjecture could then lead us, in one very special sense, perhaps to see the tale proper, which follows the ballad, as even *more* distorted. One might then well ask why we so easily assume that the first part of the tale is to be a more accurate view of the phenomena named William Budd than the account, say, titled "Billy in the Darbies."

My final point begins by asking what these digressions have in common. They are each, I would reply, a comment, an interpretation, of the early part of the tale itself—up to the point of the hanging and the mystifying paradox of the condemned man calling down the blessing of God upon the man responsible for his hanging. Moreover, each of these reactions comes clearly and intentionally from a recognizable and definable point of view, which is itself indicative of a hypothetical but nonetheless identifiable and symbolic source. The surgeon and purser, for example, represent the *scientific* and the *mercantilistic* (depending perhaps on how one classifies pursers). For these two, the phenomenal behavior of Billy— only the physiological interests them in the first place—is beyond rational explanation and thus beyond their interest. "It was phenomenal," the surgeon pedantically explains to the purser, "in the sense that it was an appearance the cause of which is not immediately to be assigned" (p. 69). The account of how petty forms were enforced on the crew following the burial is a *military* reaction to the phenomenal. Unthinking and almost instinctive subservience to authority was instituted to keep the pernicious phenomenal from affecting military efficiency and cohesiveness. The death of Captain Vere with the words "Billy Budd, Billy Budd" on his lips represents the reaction of a major *participant* in the phenomenal event. Here the reaction described is one of consciously contrived ambiguity: "That these [words] were *not* the accents of remorse *would seem* clear from what the attendant said to the *Bellipotent*'s senior officer of the marines" (p. 72, emphasis added). But we are never told what the attendant in fact said to the senior officer of the marines, only that "as the most reluctant to condemn of the members of the Drumhead court . . . he kept the knowledge to himself, who Billy Budd was" (p. 72). The newspaper account is, of course, the *journalistic* one, only apparently turning things, as we like to think journalists often do, upside down. The sailors who viewed the spar as a piece of the cross have given the phenomenal a *Christian* or mythic interpretation. Finally, the ballad, from the sailor of *artless* poetic temperament (how Melville must have enjoyed writing that phrase), is the representative of *art*. Science, mercantilism, the military, a participant, journalism, Christianity, and art—nothing less inclusive than this great sweep becomes Melville's inspired interpreters of the phenomenal Billy Budd.

Each of these interpretations, let me say in conclusion, must be viewed as at least partially true. The unintelligible and inexplicable physiological manifestation is indeed, for scientist and merchant alike, simply the manifestation of an "appearance the cause of which is not immediately to be assigned." The participant in such a phenomenal event may be assigned the role of a Pontius Pilate as well as one of a god. But whether a fated Judas, who must instigate the betrayal to precipitate the eventual resurrection, or a fated god, who must sacrifice a son in order to save a world, a role is a role; and whether assigned by fate to the diabolical or to the heavenly, whether one is to be the well-meaning dupe or the concerned humanist, that no one can ultimately know what his true role is, as the saying goes, is true enough. The journalistic account, at least in its essentials, is literally and legally true. Billy, after all, did kill a superior officer in time of war. He was, as a consequence, summarily tried and hanged. Certainly such a view is no less true than that of the sailors and the many literary critics who have followed them who have seen Billy as Jesus Christ. The marvelous view of the artist— especially when enclosed, as is the ballad, within something far more complex—is that of a marvelous and witty artist. "O, tis me, not the sentence they'll suspend"—he and his Bristol Molly. Indeed, are not the "oozy weeds" which "about [him] twist" at least as persuasive as that "vapory fleece of the Lamb of God seen in mystical vision"—the penultimate sign of the hanging scene?

No, the *truths* of the digressions, even if admittedly partial truths, are incontestable. Even if they are only partial truths which distort the whole, it is only in the comprehensive totality of those partial truths that we can begin to conceive the whole. That the whole, in another and literal sense, is itself only a part—factually speaking, the tale was incomplete when Melville died—is no more curious or ironic, or appropriate, finally, than its curious textual history as a continuously transforming account of what Melville in fact said in what he did complete. All of which fits beautifully into my thesis that *Billy Budd, Sailor* is at base a fiction about the ever-changing nature of fiction.

Its strange textual history, incidentally, has almost as many intricacies as the fiction itself. It was discovered and first published, by Raymond Weaver, in 1924, although Melville died in 1891; Weaver's edition, even as revised in 1928, was not an attempt to present all parts of the manuscript and therefore was not totally reliable; F. Barron Freeman's Harvard University Press edition of 1948, the first effort to establish a reliable text, was so filled with errors that the press (in June of 1951) temporarily withdrew the book from sale; Elizabeth Treeman, an editor for the Harvard Press, prepared a corrigenda supposedly "correcting" Freeman's errors; the Harvard Press (in June of 1953) again offered the book for sale, accompanied by Treeman's corrigenda; her corrections were worked into the edition first published in the college anthology edited by Bradley, Beatty, and Long (*The American Tradition in Literature*, 1956); and this edition was the one most widely used by scholars, critics, interpreters, adaptors (including those already mentioned here), editors, and anthologists. That three additional editions appeared in the meantime with separate and individualized collations of the Freeman-Treeman text and the manuscript and that all in one way or another committed some of the errors of the original Harvard edition merely compounds the comedy. I for one am not ready to concede that it is quite yet over, in spite of the edition researched by Hayford and Sealts and published by the University of Chicago Press in 1962. The careful and meticulous printing of that edition followed many years of painstaking labor, the application of a comprehensive and minute knowledge of all of Melville's works, the use of the latest technical knowledge about textual methods, and the employing of the skills of chirographers, cacographers, and others. It is this text that I have used here, although in 1975, well over a decade after the publication of the Chicago Press text, Milton R. Stern, a Melville scholar with credentials as impeccable as those of professors Hayford and Sealts, brought out still another edition of the text, published by the Bobbs-Merrill Company in Indianapolis, in which he reinserts into the text some of the material excluded by Hayford and Sealts!

But Weaver's earliest truncated text had ingrained in it as

deeply as do the Chicago and the Stern texts this commitment to form, as I have maintained here, that questions form.
All the texts contain the digressions. The *Billy Budd* that
ends with the hanging scene, in completeness and balance, is
certainly good enough—with that "symmetry of form attainable in pure fiction." The adaptations are sufficient testimony
to that. But the ragged edges of truth *uncompromisingly* told
(as in these greater fictions?) need forms intrinsically their
own. It is precisely this need that Melville's digressions so
precisely and so beautifully meet.

"The Birthplace": James's Fable for Critics?

I saw somewhere some years ago that ninety-five books about
Henry James were then catalogued in the Dartmouth College library. Many more than that have surely been published, perhaps more than about any other American writer.
Why this is probably so has an equally probable if perhaps
too easy answer: no critical, scholarly, historical, biographi-
cal, bibliographical, exegetical, textual, or statistical method
yet invented or discovered by man or computer has failed to
find in one aspect or another of the Jamesian world appropriate fodder off which to feed.

But even this assertion, like most assertions about James,
has its antecedents. C. Hartley Grattan in 1932 said that
James "has been praised and condemned for all the contradictory reasons any discerning and critical reader can invent
or imagine as he reads through the endless line of volumes
containing the work which for over forty years flowed from
[his] pen."[3] In such a situation it is essential to keep James
and his critics clearly separated. In this endeavor we need
look no further for guidance than to the master himself. By
this I do not mean to suggest that we consider that not insignificant portion of his domain that is itself criticism, or criticism
of criticism, or even critical theory about criticism (the cate-
gories are all nicely gathered and indexed for us in James E.
Miller, Jr.'s *Theory of Fiction: Henry James*). I mean instead

that we should look to the fiction itself, for I have long believed that we are much closer to the complex reality of any writer's works when nuzzled against his or her practice than when against his or her theory.[4]

We might, therefore, get a fresh view of the critics of James by looking at his tale on the subject of literary greatness and the vast community that feeds off it. I refer, of course, to "The Birthplace," the 1903 story of Morris Gedge, a small-town librarian who, with his wife Isabel, is made custodian and chief guide to what is identified in the story only as "the early home of the supreme poet."[5] Other characters include Grant-Jackson, spokesman for the unnamed body which has proprietorship of the shrine, who, because the Gedges had once been kind to his young son, offers them the job and oversees their performance; a Ms. Putchin, who is retiring from the post, but not before indoctrinating the new custodians into their new responsibilities; and a bright young couple from America, Mr. and Mrs. B. D. Hayes. The central characters are Morris and Isabel Gedge; ostensibly Morris is more central than Isabel, but only ostensibly, as I hope to maintain in a moment. In the tale proper Morris, becoming increasingly sensitive to the works of the unnamed poet whose birthplace the shrine is said to be, gradually refuses to lie about what is actually known, for which he is threatened with dismissal. He then perversely begins to spin vast and elaborate fabrications, for which his stipend is doubled.

Many years ago, I tied Gedge's relation to the unnamed poet to James's various specific observations about Shakespeare, especially in his then-little-known preface to an edition of *The Tempest*.[6] I then extrapolated from that "tie" (between James and Shakespeare, between Gedge and the poet) four articulated attitudes toward literary greatness that the tale then seemed to me to present: (1) that of the artistic mind (Morris Gedge's) "which is provoked into original creation" of its own; (2) "that of the purely critical mind (the Hayeses') which, while sensitive to literary achievement and indignant at the vulgarization of genius, is nonetheless itself noncreative"; (3) that of "the public mind [Grant-Jackson's, the public's, Ms. Putchin's] which exploits greatness for its own aims, whether they be narrowly materialistic or, more broadly, merely egoistic"; and (4) that of what "I [then called] the domestic mind (Isabel Gedge's) which sees clearly enough the nature of genius but nevertheless rates its worth somewhere well below conjugal security."

I have no particular desire to disavow that particular invention here—or, indeed, the several other inventions or imaginings the tale provoked before or after the appearance of mine.[7] What I want to do instead is simply supply another.

Let us arbitrarily equate for a moment, therefore, the birthplace with the James canon, every word of it that is available or might become available, and imagine, further, that the Gedges, the Hayeses, Grant-Jackson, Ms. Putchin, and the public constitute the vast community that is every reader of and every writer on Henry James and his works. What, then, is it that Henry James's fiction itself tells us about the critics of Henry James?

Let us look first at Gedge's qualification as a critic of James. He is surely all reverence for the created world itself: "He felt as if a window had opened into a great green woodland, a woodland that had a name all glorious, immortal, that was peopled with vivid figures, each of them renowned, and that gave out a murmur, deep as the sound of the sea, which was the rustle in forest shade of all the poetry, the beauty, the colour of life. It would be prodigious, that of this transfigured world *he* should keep the key" (p. 225). But simultaneously with that reverence is also the recognition of its separateness: "We shan't get it. Why should we? It's perfect" (p. 225). He is nonetheless determined to know all there is to know about the poet. "*We* must, he insists, know everything" (p. 228). He carefully, methodically, determinedly studies the works, reading them aloud, "earnestly commenting and collating" (p. 229). The poet's world, for a time, literally becomes his—a "personal friend," a "universal light," a "final authority and divinity" (p. 229). Indeed, in his heady intoxication at this point, at which he is said to be "all possession and comprehension and sympathy," he is led to state that it is "absurd" to talk any longer of "not knowing. So far as we don't," he continues, "it's because we're dunces. He's *in* the thing, over His ears, and the more we get into it the more we're with Him. I seem to myself at any rate," he declared, "to *see* Him in it as if He were painted on the wall" (p. 230).

It is here that Isabel breaks in to agree, but with a significant difference. "We see Him," she says, "because we love

Him—that's what we do. How can we not, the old darling, with what He's doing for us?" When Morris replies that he even sees, "confound me, the faults," Isabel retorts: "That's because you're so critical. You see them, but you don't mind them. You see them, but you forgive them." But of course, she goes on, in the first big twist to the tale, "you mustn't mention them." "Dear no," Morris laughingly replies. "We'll chuck out anyone who hints at them."

What more devoted Jamesian could one ask for than Gedge?

But he learns all too quickly that such intimate and familiar and informed knowledge as he possesses is not at all what the public wants, is not what Ms. Putchin had instructed him it wanted, is not what Grant-Jackson, as spokesman for the body, will permit him to teach it as what it should want. All this is hardly new, incidentally, to Isabel.

With the arrival on the scene at this point of the two sensitive young critics from America, the Hayeses, we find a view that reveals more interest in Gedge's dilemma about the poet than in the poet himself. To be sure, they share Gedge's reverence for the subject; they share his indignation at the prostitution, as Gedge sees it, of the poet's shrine; and although they disagree with Gedge in seeing the desecration of the man as carrying with it the necessary desecration of the work,[8] they also share with Gedge the delightful irony in the intrinsic beauty of his ultimately contrived, elaborate, and artful fabrications. They do not, however, share Gedge's great facility, although it is Ms. Hayes who in fact first names it—"You're really a genius" (p. 268)—who brings word to Gedge of his American fame, and who specifically describes the end to which Gedge at last finds himself driven to have been a thrust upward rather than downward. "Up a different tree," to be sure, as Mr. Hayes concretely puts it, "but . . . up at the tip-top" nevertheless (p. 247).

What body or bodies of Jamesian criticism the Hayeses might be said to represent is difficult to say. It is, of course, a distinctly American criticism and is therefore judged to be, however acute and sensitive and even generous,[9] of a lower, less significant order than that represented by Gedge himself.

My final point in this little fable for critics locates an order that is, to me, higher than that represented by either the Hayeses, or by Gedge himself. For Isabel's position subsumes the whole question of poet and critic, affirms values more central to the human condition than those of aesthetic or literary history, embodies, in short, a position about human need and common sense that questions the very need for aesthetic worth. Isabel, not Morris, is ultimately responsible for the custodial triumph: it was she who had years before nursed back to health the son of the great Grant-Jackson, that "tiniest and tenderest of her husband's pupils" (p. 230), and thus had first established the tie that led to their appointment. She, moreover, is the person who describes "true affection" (p. 230) as reflecting the greatest "light" there is. And she is no fool, even though Gedge at one place describes her as no more than one of "Them." She in fact possesses every faculty that her husband possesses—and more. She is everywhere said to be as sensitive to the poet as is Gedge. Her power to prevaricate is demonstrably as great as his,[10] literally said to be "stupendous" at one spot (p. 259). She is the one who first tells her husband that he has a high critical faculty (p. 230); who tells him later that the bottom of the heap is the place for such a faculty in a position such as theirs; and who at least has the perception to know that Gedge, conceivably, could "dish them by too much romance as well as by too little" (p. 268). She clearly sees her husband's sensitivity, his obsession, his great facility, and sees them in the order of their importance. But she never confuses herself with the poet, in drawing "rather sharply the line between her own precinct and that in which the great spirit might walk" (p. 237). It would be hard, ultimately, to deny her charge, early in the tale, that "common sense, which the vulgar have less than anything, . . . must be as wanted [at the shrine? with the works?] as . . . anywhere else" (p. 277).

I have already suggested how in my earlier invention about "The Birthplace" I used much of this same evidence to read Isabel's role as one representing mere "conjugal security" or "domestic peace." In this invention, it serves my fancy to see it much more centrally: it presents at least one Jamesian conception that values literary criticism, however impassioned, resourceful, sensitive, or, indeed, imaginative and regenerative, somewhere below quite simple, quite commonplace, human virtue. The irony with which the whimsy, the comedy, or the cynicism might be said to accompany Gedge's rescue at the end of this fable is no irony at all in contrast to a view of literary criticism that can meaningfully touch the world off which it feeds *only* when it itself becomes a subject through which or by which simple human value is established.

We are thus back somewhere near where we started. Having moved through or by one little excursive rubric from the fiction, we still find the Jamesian world all inviolate, untouched, still somehow magnificently *there*, on one side, and the vast community of James readers and critics on the other. The criticism ultimately touches the fiction no more than the fiction touches—to squeeze in one small allusion to the current faddish concern with mimesis—the so-called "real" world. Should the criticism thus be discarded? Not at all, no more, at any rate, than the fiction should be. But let us begin to take it for what it is: another world all its own, fattening, to be sure, on the works as the exclusive energizing nutrient, in many languages and rhythms; serving a multiplicity of purposes for a multiplicity of reasons, magnificently varied, detailed, banal, repetitious, complex, erudite, expansive, anything, in short, one wants to make of it; and somehow inexplicably growing as it has never grown before.[11] But however corpulent that criticism is or ultimately becomes and however voluminous the criticism James himself composed about his fiction and that of others, the inviolable distinctions between the artist and the critic I see so clearly marked in "The Birthplace" are likely to be, indeed, should be, maintained.

Faulkner's Revolt against the 1920s: Parody and Transcendence, Continuation and Innovation

When Ernest Hemingway referred to Faulkner's great Yoknapatawpha as "Anomatopoeio County" (he had earlier called it "Octonawhoopoo"); when he said that no mere county was big enough to hold him, that the Gulf Stream was his domain, and that fighting marlin, not catfish, was his game[12]— he could not have known how that derisively labeled locale contained an intricate, profound, and significant comment on his own fictional world (and those of his fellow writers of the 1920s). To be sure, Hemingway elsewhere had many fine things to say about Faulkner, as did Faulkner about Hemingway, in contrastive moods perhaps equally irascible and adulatory. But my interest here is not with the public jockeying of these two; it is instead with Faulkner's revolt against the 1920s, especially the Faulkner of *The Sound and the Fury* of 1929, *As I Lay Dying* of 1930, and *Light in August* of 1932. For the three together, it seems to me, are not only comments on the literary achievements and preoccupations of some of the decade's major American writers and those who influenced them; they are also Faulkner's curiously envisioned adaptations of those preoccupations to his own developing artistic needs. The three novels are of course significant enough when seen as separate things-in-themselves or in their own context as a Faulknerian trilogy. But when also seen in the context of literary history, of continuity, of ties, links, and developments, we get a perspective that helps to define their achievement *within* a tradition. Faulkner's mode, I will contend, is parody (external and internal). The result is continuation and innovation—continuation through parodic replication of some of the more daring themes and techniques of the 1920s; innovation through audacious transformation of those same themes and techniques.

Hence, the year 1929 might be said to end the decade not because of the stock-market crash or even because of the publication of *A Farewell to Arms* (Hemingway's last important novel until 1941) but because of the publication of *The Sound and the Fury*, a novel that ends a tradition by fulfilling it, even as that fulfillment becomes a new literary experimentation of its own. The complex achievement of that novel is the great mystery of Faulkner's career; nothing in his previous work quite foretold it. To be sure, there is plenty that is imitative of the 1920s in both *Soldier's Pay* and *Mosquitoes*, his precounty apprentice novels, as many critics have remarked.[13] Even his first county novel, *Sartoris* (or *Flags in the Dust*), with all the development that it represents in first locating for Faulkner that little postage-stamp area of Northern Mississippi that was so successfully to feed his developing imagination, is also often described as depicting a world reminiscent of those in *The Waste Land* or in *The Sun Also Rises*. Although other aspects of *Flags in the Dust* are indeed predictive of later development in Faulkner—the magnificent Snopes trilogy, for example—nothing in it intelligibly foreshadows the audacious assault that *The Sound and the Fury* makes upon the literary sensibilities of the time.

The focus there on the death of a world through the fall of a family, the aristocratic Compsons, is most memorable, of course, through its technique of filtering the story through the sensibilities of the three Compson brothers—the idiot Benjy, the sensitive but ultimately suicidal Quentin, and the greedy, petty-minded Jason. The brilliant variety of rubrics by which this triad of points of view can be seen is truly legendary, as I have previously remarked.[14] Central to all these rubrics, however, is the elemental tie of the inadequacy of each to the simple challenge of their sister Caddy's at least comparatively normal growth. Their innocence in confrontation with Caddy's "experience" thus becomes the novel's subject and its technique. Each of the Compson brothers is a narrator and tale-teller; each is also a participant, a character. Hence, the concepts of narration that each represents, although brilliantly varied, are nevertheless linked and tied within a context of theme and technique as practiced by some of the major novelists of the 1920s.

Let me be boldly direct at this point. The Benjy section reflects most centrally a Hemingway tradition of the 1920s, especially that embodied by Jake Barnes. The Quentin section is tied to T. S. Eliot—and to Joyce. The Jason section recalls Sinclair Lewis. Parody controls each rendition. Finally, the Dilsey section is foil to them all—to their modes and tones no less than to their compulsive conditions. Innocence links the Compsons—until foiled by Dilsey. And a kind of innocence links these writers of the 1920s—until foiled by Faulkner.

This, of course, is all much too explicit and direct, not necessarily, I would concede, even the result of any fully conscious and central intention on Faulkner's part, and not, moreover, in any prescriptive way exhaustive or depletive among the compound levels of *The Sound and the Fury*. Yet, there is some clearly cohering sense of this relation between Faulkner's novel and the writers of the decade that I have mentioned.

Among the many ramifications of this contention is the recognition of the crucial role Benjy plays among the novel's narrative voices. No one questions anymore the position that Benjy, Quentin, and Jason are more alike than unalike, or that Benjy, although the last of the sons, is given to us as the first because he is indeed the primal, innermost core, the center pole, as it were, around which the more sophisticated concepts of his brothers are wrapped and shaped, or that his perspective is, at base, the most direct, the most pure, however much we initially think the opposite. Born an idiot, "mindless at birth," he is, Faulkner has literally told us regarding his conception, one of "the truly innocent."[15]

So, of course, is Jake Barnes, as Mark Spilka demonstrated in his "The Death of Love in *The Sun Also Rises*."[16] But perhaps the more telling evidence of a possible relationship between these two innocent narrators is in their intricate and suggestive parallels (unlike, say, the more obvious thematic ties of both *Soldier's Pay* and *Flags in the Dust* to Hemingway's war fiction): Benjy's emasculation and Jake's phallic wound; their objective, restrictive reporting of the worlds they see around them; their mutual focus on apparently promiscuous women (Caddy and Lady Brett); and, most important for me, the stylistic analogues of their deceptively simple, seemingly direct, almost photographic modes of expression—most often through dropped modification and enjambment. When these parallels are capped with the demonstration by John M. Howell of the astounding similarities of context, action, diction, and syntax between a scene of Jake "in his bedroom agonizing over Brett" and one of Benjy "in his bedroom agonizing over Caddy," I am persuaded to accept the purported connection.[17] Concepts of disjointed time and images of grotesque gardens viewed through "empty . . . blue eyes" which Howell cites as allusions to Fitzgerald's *Gatsby* are for me less persuasive. But Fitzgerald's concepts of innocence *are* within the bounds of Faulkner's theme, as are those in the Eliotic mode, especially its Prufrockian strain, that have often enough been noticed—by Michael Millgate and others, for example—as reflected in the self-narrated account of Quentin's ridiculous suicide in the second section *and* in the Sinclair Lewis–inspired Babbittry apparent in the conception of Jason in the third.[18]

Collectively, then, these parodic allusions to writers as disparate as Hemingway, Eliot, Lewis, and possibly Fitzgerald become a part of the connected total structure of *The Sound and the Fury*, wherein the idiot Benjy is the pivotal key: conceived and rendered as he is to radiate slyly backward toward Hemingway and possibly Fitzgerald (but clearly toward Hemingway's style), to function effectively within the confines of the novel's own need as a comically grotesque yet elegiacally moving mode of narration and of theme, and also to radiate forward to accruing concepts as embodied in Quentin and Jason, whose own differing, yet linked manifestations of innocent narration *themselves* become retrospective looks at still other writers of the 1920s. "The great strength" of the 1920s, concluded Frederick J. Hoffman in his still-standard study of the decade, is "its useful and deliberate innocence,"[19] a concept Faulkner appears not only fully to have understood but also (if somewhat mockingly) fully to have appropriated.

Faulkner's release, however, is as sure as his grasp; for when, in the final section of the novel, he foils the failures of the brothers through the staying power of the wise and positive Dilsey, when he foils their intricate modes of tale-telling with old-fashioned omniscient narration and relatively straightforward structure, his mockery has its perfect cap. That the modes of the fourth section might also be somewhat reminiscent of the old plantation novel, replete with Negro "Mammy," only adds to the fun. Even so, the central force of the novel is not one of comedy but of tragedy, not of gain but of pain—the universal moan, as it were, over the loss of innocence.

In his next novel comedy *is* the overt mode, but covert parody is still at play, perhaps most centrally, as parody of self, or at least that part of the self that is the eloquent despair of *The Sound and the Fury*. But perhaps external parody is still operable too. *As I Lay Dying*, like its predecessor, is a tale of the trials and tribulations of a Southern family, but this time it focuses on poor whites from the back country, not the aristocratic Compsons of the town. It is not, moreover, a tale of the dissolution of a family but one of a family's growth and solidification. While it is a tale of death, to be sure, it is death seen as regeneration, not degeneration. The protagonist (I will argue briefly for Anse in a moment) appears to be everything that a husband and father should *not* be, but this is only appearance. Its brilliant monologues, the totally original way that they are used to render this riotous, macabre, and yet heroic account of Addie Bundren's husband and five children on their "odyssey" to Jefferson with Addie's dead, putrefying body, and the Biblical and literary overlays (Is Anse in some ways a Joycean "Molly" figure, Addie the "Bloom" one?) are all without parallel in our literature. For everywhere in the novel the comic inversions explode with rich contradictions; any speaker's apparent meanings are always rife with possible opposite interpretations; the major action itself is simultaneously heroic and absurd.

In Addie's great monologue, for example, she discusses the implacable and invidious distinction between words and deeds and designates Anse as a word man, too much a nothing even to know that he was not alive, so much a nothing that the only image she can dredge up to suggest what he is to her is an empty door-frame, just a shape to fill a lack. Yet in one clear sense Anse can be seen to be what Addie considers herself to be, a person of action, a doer, and Addie herself to be the devotee of words that she describes Anse as being. After all, Addie's extraction of a promise to bury her in Jefferson and Anse's carrying it out constitute the central movement of the novel. Moreover, Addie is the philosopher and analyst and introspective introvert; Anse is the one who propels the action, who gets things done, and who says very little (his great true line, "You and me," he tells Addie, "ain't nigh done chapping yet, with just two," notwithstanding). Late in the book, when Cash, the sanest of all the Bundrens— sane because he cuts joints on the bevel and thus perhaps joins Addie's never-meeting horizontals and verticals?—is told by Dr. Peabody that the only bright spot he can imagine in Cash's broken leg is the fact that it is the same leg he has previously broken and is thus still left with one good limb, Cash's significant reply is "That's what Pa says." Much, too, could be said about Anse's resourcefulness at the end of the novel. He does, after all, provide his motherless children with a new Mrs. Bundren, duck shaped and popeyed though she is. Moreover, she is the owner of a graphophone even if she is also the one from whom Anse had borrowed the shovel with which to dig Addie's grave! Serious laughter inevitably results, insane comedy, to be sure, but, simultaneously, sane, elemental affirmation.

Such affirmation, moreover, not only foils its opposite in

the Compsons; it perhaps also foils the more comprehensive despair of the writers of the 1920s. Its absurd play with point of view—Addie's great monologue coming in time within the novel after her death, Darl's third-person description of himself being carried off to the insane asylum in his last scene, the absence of any clearly defined center to the novel's multiple voices—is, in a way, experimentation run mad but also possibly a comment, through his own more limited use of the technique in *The Sound and the Fury*, about such experimentation in general. When, finally, we recall the novel's hyperbolic play with myths—Biblical ones as with the fire and flood, classical ones as with the rites of burial, and, most significant, literary ones as most explicitly keyed to Joyce's Molly Bloom in Darl's "Yes, yes, yes, yes . . ." as *his* final words—we see in *As I Lay Dying* a Faulkner who could be as playful with that great influence on the 1920s, the author of *Ulysses* (and perhaps other myth-exploiters), as he had earlier shown himself to be with Hemingway, Fitzgerald, Eliot, and Lewis.

Light in August, the last of my examples, is a neat brief capstone to my thesis. Here is a clear-cut repudiation of the experimental methodologies that mockingly tied its two predecessors to the 1920s. But we also see its singular affirmation, continuation, if you like, of a central thematic thrust of each of those two earlier works. In *Light in August* Faulkner makes no recourse to difficult, ambiguous participating narrators, to limited points of view, to variations on the device of the monologue, or to involved stream-of-consciousness techniques. Its story line is more or less direct, its point of view omniscient, its structuring tactics at least comparatively simple. Even so, its bifurcated centers of interest—the framing Lena Grove and the encircled and circling Joe Christmas—are at base replications of the themes of *As I Lay Dying* and *The Sound and the Fury*. The comic yes, yes, yes of the Bundren saga *and* the tragic no, no, no of the Compson one are here brought together and mutually affirmed. These contrastive yet complementary concepts can, to be sure, also be seen in other terms, especially as what Lena and Joe come to represent is controlled and modified through the interlocking tales of Byron Bunch, Gail Hightower, and Joanna Burden, concepts such as light and dark, life and death, movement and stasis, affirmation and denial. But even these terms are not inappropriate ones to describe the contrastive thematic thrusts of those two earlier works.

When, therefore, at the end of *Light in August* we see as inexorably continuing in the world both the comedy that is Lena Grove and the tragedy that is Joe Christmas, the emotive and the rational, as it were, irreconcilably but nonetheless mutually affirmed, we are also meant to see the irreconcilable itself posed as both the human glory *and* the human burden, one no less important, no less there, than the other—a view of the human condition, in short, encompassed by *As I Lay Dying* and *The Sound and the Fury* when their values are seen collectively as unequivocally coequal.

It is in such an inclusive recapitulation that I, at any rate, see a contextual relationship of *Light in August* to these two predecessors. Moreover, it is their parodic relationship to writers and movements within the 1920s that marks so brilliantly Faulkner's ties to the decade and, as capped by the daringly different narrative mode of *Light in August*, his progressively direct revolt against it. That so much of the literature of the 1920s was both captured and transcended by Faulkner, captured and transcended, moreover, in so compact, so compressed a manner—not only within the unlikely confines of that mythical county of Northern Mississippi that Hemingway so derisively called Octonawhoopoo but within the even more compact and compressed confines of these three novels[20]—is one of the literary wonders of our time. Such audacious effrontery could only emit from a supremely self-confident, knowledgeable, and still expanding literary imagination.

Thus did Faulkner make his bow to the 1920s even as he dismissed them, employing their tactics, themes, and strategies even as he denied them and affirmed his own. His very life during that decade, let me finish here as a kind of coda, was even a kind of parody: RCAF service, but too late to go to war; the swaggering return home, replete with polished puttees, Sam Browne belt, and swagger stick, *and* with flyer's wings that he had never earned; expatriation—mini-fashion, not to Paris, but to the local Southern version of Paris, New Orleans (his 1925 visit to Europe notwithstanding); and, finally, an exile's return, but only to that little postage-stamp area of Northern Mississippi he knew so well.

SEVEN

Afterword

"Knower, Doer, and Sayer"—
The James Family View of Emerson

When i first published my findings of the views of the James family toward Ralph Waldo Emerson in 1953, I did so under the simple title of "Emerson and the James Family."[1] I here propose to reformulate those earlier findings, examine their staying power, and "test" (as it were, and insofar as I can) the extent to which this earliest and most un-self-conscious example of my "method" in this diverse collection of essays has any current validity. Would I, in short, on reflection, crucially change or qualify my earlier-held convictions about the attitudes of the elder Henry James and his two famous sons, William and Henry, toward Emerson? Would I express myself differently? Would I discover, among the voluminous scholarship devoted to these four writers during the past twenty-seven years, new material, new insights, new configurations to that particular context?

I began my original essay with F. O. Matthiessen's assertion that "the comments" of the James family "upon Emerson compose by themselves a chapter of American intellectual history."[2] Three near-contemporaries of widely differing tastes (I then asserted), although all members of a single remarkably intellectual American family, viewed the writings and life of Emerson in radically different ways. I designated the elder Henry James and his sons Henry and William as, respectively, a theologian, an artist, and a philosopher. As my central thesis I proclaimed that although each James saw Emerson only partially, taken as a unit, they saw him whole—according to Emerson's own definition of a whole man.

It is no longer necessary to explain or defend these arbitrary designations for each of the Jameses, given their now much better known careers and, indeed, the perspective each took toward Emerson. Nor is it necessary to recount again how when Emerson lectured in New York on "The Times" on 3 March 1842, Henry James, Sr., heard him and, with characteristic candor, wrote him a letter praising his lecture, albeit with some reservations, and invited Emerson to come see him, which Emerson promptly did (*JF*, pp. 39–40), thereby beginning a lifelong friendship between the two that eventually encompassed all members of both families.

My original and much more extensive "case" ran essentially as follows:

Emerson as "Knower"

The *sustained* element in the elder Henry James's interest in Emerson was with his personal qualities, with Emerson the man, not with Emerson the writer. Such, at any rate, was my original reading of the thirty-three-year correspondence between the two, as supported by the two essays James wrote about his friend.[3] Such was not the reading given by the numerous earlier commentators on the relationship between the two,[4] a somewhat surprising discovery, it seemed to me, given the evidence.

James's own retrospective view of his correspondence with Emerson was memorably caught in a late-life letter to James Elliot Cabot, who had requested permission to quote from it in the *Memoir* on Emerson that he was then preparing.

> I cannot flatter myself that any letter I ever wrote to Emerson is worth reading. . . . Emerson always kept one at such arm's length, tasting him and sipping him and trying him, to make sure that he was worthy of his somewhat prim and bloodless friendship, that it was fatiguing to write him letters. . . . I remember well what maidenly letters I used to receive from him, with so many tentative charms of expression in them that if he had been a woman one would have delighted in complimenting him. . . . It is painful to recollect now the silly hope that I had, along the early days of our acquaintance, that if I went on listening, something would be sure to drop from him that would show me an infallible way out of his perplexed world. For nothing ever came but epigrams; sometimes clever, sometimes not.[5]

This somewhat cantankerous view of their correspondence is nevertheless, according to Ralph Leslie Rusk, editor of Emerson's letters, not an inaccurate view of their respective tones.[6] The correspondence had begun, however, on a much more hopeful and expectant note. Even so, in his very first letter we find the germinal dichotomy upon which James interpreted Emerson for the rest of his life: Emerson's apparent indifference to intellect, on the one hand, and his sincerity of purpose, "that erect attitude of mind" (Perry, 1:40), on the other. A fascination with Emerson's personality coupled with an intrinsic distrust of his intuitive flights is, in short, the anomaly at the center of the elder Henry James's lifelong view of Emerson.

Emerson's apparent distrust of intellect bothered James from the very first. It was for James "the necessary digestive apparatus" of his life. In an undated letter of 1842, the year he met Emerson, he complained that "you continually dishearten me . . . by the dishonor you seem to cast upon our intelligence, as if it stood much in our way" (Perry, 1:40). This complaint was to run through much of their correspondence, reaching perhaps its most vivid expression in his good-natured (and well-known) expostulation following, as James viewed it, Emerson's refusal to "explain" or "defend" his point of view: "Oh you man without a handle! shall one never be able to help himself out of you, according to his needs, and be dependent only upon your fitful tippings-up?" (Perry, 1:40).

Concurrently, however, he retained a perplexing fascination with Emerson's personality and character, which held a promise, it seemed to James, somehow suggestive of an almost absolute perfection. Although James was later to describe their positions as exactly polarized—"What he mainly held to be true I could not help regarding as false, and what he mainly held to be false I regarded as true" ("Emerson," p. 740)—he nonetheless saw in Emerson some ineffably personal attraction, an intuitive pull somehow so persuasive that it became the dominant factor in James's interpretation of his friend. James was particularly eloquent, and vivid, in his description of this charm in Emerson's lectures, the almost palpable "presence" there "of a positive personal grace," a charm "intensely personal," James reiterates, and "exquisitely characteristic" ("Emerson," p. 741). Still, it was a promise that Emerson's intellect, for James, did not fulfill.

James was later to fit this hope/frustration evaluation into his own theological system. Meanwhile, his friendship with Emerson continued. Emerson had described him enthusiastically both to his wife and Margaret Fuller (Rusk, 3:23, 30). He loaded James with introductions to his friends in Europe, including Carlyle (Perry, 1:49), asked him to arrange for lecture halls in New York (Rusk, 4:184), sent Thoreau to visit him,[7] introduced him to other New England friends, and on at least one occasion invited him to lecture before the Town and Country Club in Boston (Rusk, 4:169). James in the meantime had fixed and focused his own theological system. Having overtly rejected Calvinism, although he in fact retained a large residuum of that faith, his discovery of the writings of Swedenborg and Fourier did not so much convert him as simply confirm and sustain him, "giving him a language," according to R. B. Perry, "a systematic frame work, and an organized support for the faith that was in him" (Perry, 1:20). But perhaps his system, especially as it was distinguished from Emerson's, is best understood as explained by his philosopher son, William. His father, explained William, "was a theologian of the 'twice-born' type, an out-and-out Lutheran, who believed that the moral law existed solely to fill us with loathing for the idea of our own merits, and to make us turn to God's grace as our only opportunity." But grace, William went on, was not to come to the isolated individual: "the sphere of redemption was *Society*." And in a "divinely" organized Society, "our natures will not be altered, but our spontaneities, because they will then work harmoniously, will all work innocently, and the Kingdom of Heaven will have come." With such ideas, said William, his father was thus both "fascinated and baffled by his friend Emerson." Emerson's "personal graces" seemed to "prefigure the coming millennium," but "the resolute individualism of his thought set my father's philosophy at defiance." No man, for James, was "superior to another." Emerson, concluded William, was a " 'once-born' man; he . . . recognized no need of a redemptive process."[8] Emerson's counterreactions made these intrinsic antagonisms even more apparent, as when, in reference to James's *Moralism and Christianity*, he objected to its "argumentative style" and to James's refusal, as Emerson saw it, to make authoritative statements, a necessity for "one broaching matters so vital and dear" (Perry, 1:62).

The two nevertheless remained intimate and friendly, although James, as he became more socially conscious, more convinced of social progress, became even less sympathetic toward Emerson's ideas. At the same time, he was still fascinated with Emerson's personality, could still see him as "the best and most memorable" of men, and would write him directly that whether "the computation begin from my heart or my head . . . your life is a very real divine performance . . . and a still fuller prophecy" (Perry, 1:80). In that continued attraction, James began to place Emerson in his own scheme as an *unconscious* embodiment of what he saw as the new social redemption of man through the simple medium of his character and personality.

James's continued distrust of Emerson's intellect is everywhere apparent in his objections to particular books by his friend. To be sure, he dismissed *English Traits* simply because, unlike his son, he could not abide English exclusiveness and complacency (Perry, 1:122–23). Although more tolerant toward *Representative Men*, because he perceived that Emerson honored great men for their human substance, their representativeness of finite traits, he could nonetheless say elsewhere that it was the little nobodies who "let the Lord shine through them without an excessive clouding of his splendour," not "pretentious somebodies" like "Plato or Emerson or Washington"![9] The playful exaggeration notwithstanding, in James's system no man was superior to another in the final plan, and the unpretentious more often reflected the divine than did the great. Finally, he was invidiously to contrast Emerson's *Society and Solitude* with his earliest two collections of essays, seeing the two sets as reflecting "youth and age, or promise and fulfilment, the former leaving something to the imagination, the latter excluding it." The "tender enthusiasm" in the sunrise, he concluded, is more exciting than what he found in the sunset, however intrinsically "admirable" both were (Perry, 1:100–101).

Considerably more caustic, however, is a well-known letter of 1868 to his son William, wherein James reiterated his old dilemma: his exasperation with Emerson's inability to communicate intellectually, "his ignorance of everything above the senses," and his paradoxical fascination with Emerson's personality. "I love the man very much, he is such a born natural." He nonetheless denigrated Emerson's attitude toward nature, called him a mere "police spy upon it," and charged his "intellectual offspring" of loving, not nature itself, but only to imitate him and say "similar 'cute' things about nature and man" (Perry, 1:90). "His books," he concluded, "are to me wholly destitute of spiritual flavour, being at most carbonic acid gas and *water*" (Perry, 1:96–97).[10]

Acid though this relatively late judgment was, it was not inconsistent with James's earlier attitude toward Emerson. James's distrust of Emerson's intellect, his indifference to dialectic (as James viewed it), and his dependence upon intuition and inspiration had been lifelong. He had written Emerson directly as early as 1849 that "I never read you as an author at all. Your books are not literature, but life, and criticism always strikes me, therefore, as infinitely laughable when applied to you" (Perry, 1:58). All of which simply throws into still higher relief James's appreciation of Emerson the man. This appreciation was unchanged throughout their lives; with the single exception of a brief public disagreement over the intellectual worth of Fourier,[11] the two remained on good terms until they died.

The gist of the first of the two formal essays that James wrote about Emerson (although published later [1904]) has been interpolated into this survey of the correspondence. The more succinct one, written some· nine years after the first (1881, the year before James died) and first published in *The Literary Remains of the Late Henry James* (1884), not only provides a neat corroborating cap to the correspondence but also makes the explicit charge that his friend lacked a sense of evil, an opinion growing out of James's conviction that Emerson, as F. O. Matthiessen has pointed out, was in an arrested state of innocence, completely impervious, in the Blakean sense, to experience (*JF*, p. 428).

James began his essay with the observation that Emerson did not have a consciousness and that that was the secret of his fascination for men. He conceded that Emerson comprehended the outward or moral difference between good and evil. But in James's system, it was the inner, individualized realization of evil that was important, a conviction of one's own unworthiness that was crucial. These formed the necessary base upon which James fixed his belief in redeemed man as a social form; the rejection of one's individualized self was as a step toward being reborn *in society*. Emerson, James was convinced, was totally bereft of any conviction of personal sin. Possessed himself of such a sense, James first viewed Emerson with a kind of astonished joy at meeting so much innocence and goodness, hoping therefrom to discover how one "got that way." But to his amazement and chagrin, James charged, Emerson had no idea that he was innocent. Emerson's superiority was all personal or practical, "acquired by birth or genius," but by no means "intellectual."

Emerson the man thus eventually came to symbolize for James a kind of divine spirit. *True* innocence, for James,

attached itself only to what was universally unindividual-
ized in our nature. It was appropriated by individuals only
insofar as they denuded themselves of personality or self-
consciousness. James concluded this essay with Christ's ad-
monition that "he that findeth his life shall lose it, and he
that loseth his life for my sake shall find it" (*JF*, pp. 435–38),
which may be roughly translated into the Jamesian system
as he who loses his innocence *in and for society* shall regain
it. Emerson, for James, was never aware of his innocence;
he therefore neither lost nor found it. He somehow simply
was it.

Although it has been said of the elder James, and with
some accuracy, that he was "one of the very few intellectual
associates of Emerson who was not an Emersonian,"[12] his
oblique insight illuminates a little-regarded aspect of Emerson that is peculiarly appropriate to Emerson's own point of
view. To see divine attributes reflected in the personality and
character of an individual whose ideas are unintelligible is
perhaps less magnanimous than penetrating. That James
the theologian saw reflected in Emerson the man a peculiar
divinity is a subtle tribute that is perhaps a juster evaluation
than one might at first realize.

Emerson as "Doer"

Henry James, Jr., the novelist, was also an astute Emersonian
critic. An awareness of "the great Emerson's" presence in his
father's household was one of his earliest and most memorable impressions. As he matured, the younger Henry James,
like his father, felt that the evil and sin of the world was "a
side of life to which Emerson's eyes were thickly bandaged"
(*JF*, p. 451). Unlike his father, however, he did not find Emerson unintelligible. He was, in fact, all too eager to "explain"
him. He was to do so, moreover, from a perspective exclusively his own, complementary though it turned out to be to
his father's views.

It was "the great Emerson—I knew he was great, greater
than any of our friends"—that James the novelist first remembers, the Concord "visitor" who was "consentingly

housed" in his father's New York home when James was a boy. His late-life account was of one whom he had known even then to command "a tone alien, beautifully alien, to any we had roundabout," one who somehow, James said, had led him, to "know myself as never yet, as I was not indeed to know myself again for years, in touch with the wonder of Boston."[13] The two touched more remotely when the young writer first began publishing his tales; then Emerson asked the elder James to "thank your boy Harry for . . . his good stories" (Rusk, 5:514). When, two years later (1869), the elder James confided to his son that he had been sharing with Emerson Henry's descriptive letters from Europe, the young novelist described himself as "terribly agitated by the thought that Emerson likes them" (Perry, 1:311).

But James was not at all "agitated" ten years later when, in his study of Hawthorne, he looked at Emerson with more detachment. His earliest view that Emerson was "alien" to the New York environment did not blind him to the naturalness of Emerson's affinity with the Concord milieu. "In a society in which introspection . . . played almost the part of a social resource," there must have been "great charm" for those who placed such "value" on the individual whose "duty" was "living by one's own light and carrying out one's own disposition." The sincerity, independence, and spontaneity insisted upon by Emerson was indeed, thought James, a "beautiful irony" upon the "exquisite impudence" (presumably located elsewhere) of institutionalized purveyors of truth. But there was a perhaps deeper irony in his tough recognition that, even within the confines of Concord, "Emerson, as a sort of spiritual sun-worshipper, could have attached but a moderate value to Hawthorne's catlike faculty of seeing in the dark."[14]

In his next extended attention to Emerson, his review of the Carlyle-Emerson correspondence in 1883, he was even more explicit in his belief that Emerson's "noble conception of good" was not balanced with a "definite conception of evil." Emerson's letters, moreover, came off badly in comparison with Carlyle's. Emerson "had not an abundant epistolary impulse. . . . His letters are less natural, more composed, have too studied a quaintness." Still, he could see both men possessed "of the poetic quality"; they were both "men of imagination" who "set above everything else the importance of conduct" and who "had the desire, the passion, for something better . . . an interest in the destiny of mankind."[15]

In his even more extended review of Cabot's *A Memoir of Ralph Waldo Emerson* (in 1887), he was piqued that Emerson was insufficiently seen mise en scène. Too little was done, thought James, with "the social conditions in which Emerson moved, the company he lived in, the moral air he breathed." For James, Emerson could only have become Emerson through particularized New England progenitors, those who "had lived long . . . in the same corner" of that region and who had "preached and studied and prayed and practiced" there. "A conscience like Emerson's," he wrote, "could not have been turned off . . . from one generation to another." James also deplored Cabot's only cursory attention to Emerson's contemporaries. To the novelist that time and place were representative and significant—"a subject bringing into play many odd figures, many human incongruities," abounding "in illustration of the primitive New England character . . . during the time of its queer search for something to expend itself upon" (*JF*, pp. 439–45, passim).

Finally, in these comments about the representative value of Emerson, James pointed to Emerson to disparage, although with gentle irony, the idea that America had no respect for literary men. "In what other country," James asked, "on sleety winter nights, would provincial and bucolic populations have gone forth in hundreds for the cold comfort of literary discourse?" No scholar, he pointed out, had ever been more revered in his lifetime than Emerson, and he called his funeral "a popular manifestation, the most striking I have ever seen provoked by the death of a man of letters" (*JF*, pp. 447–48).

But the more central issue, of course, is James's view of Emerson's writings, his view of Emerson as a man of letters. The central assessment was a curiously ambivalent one. On the one hand, he was convinced that Emerson "never really mastered the art of composition." He never acquired a complex concept of form. His remark that Emerson had but "one style, one manner, and he had it for everything—even for himself in his notes and journals" was disparagement, however gentle. He even charged Emerson with excessive circumlocution in his habit of "hovering round and round an idea." On the other hand, "it was only because [Emerson] was so deferential that he could be so detached," practicing "a kind of unusual passive hospitality." Because James could not subscribe to the Emersonian concept that talent was inferior to inspiration, he could only conclude that Emerson was an exception to "the general rule that writings live in the last resort by their form." The exception was crucial, however, for it led James to conclude that a deficiency in style—"usually the bribe or toll-money on the journey to posterity" (*JF*, pp. 445–47, 452–53)—made Emerson's accomplishments all the more striking.

Like his father, James felt the force of Emerson's personal magnetism, his somehow possessing "the equanimity of a result; nature had [so] taken care of him [that] he had only to speak." Also like his father, James perceived Emerson somehow to be "the prayer and the sermon . . . in his own subtle insinuating way a sanctifier." But not at all like the father's was the son's conviction that Emerson's "great distinction, . . . his special sign," was his possession of "a more vivid conception of the moral life than anyone else." The younger James could even describe his "ripe unconsciousness of evil" as "one of the most beautiful signs by which we know him." Emerson's "genius for seeing character as. a real and supreme thing" (*JF*, pp. 441–42) was strikingly acute.

James concluded this essay with the judgment that Emerson had been unsurpassed in his ability to speak "to the soul in a voice of direction and authority." However varied and numerous the competing "voices," ended James, none other had "just that firmness and just that purity" (*JF*, p. 452).

Matthiessen has written that James's late-life revisit and reseeing of his homeland, as recorded in *The American Scene* (1907), was as though James "had explicitly decided [therein] to be Emerson's 'transparent eyeball' and nothing else."[16] The almost ineffable Emersonian residuum in James, however, was more clearly seen in that volume in his memorable apostrophe to the village of Concord. Surely it was mostly Emerson he was addressing when he rhetorically declared that "there are so many places, 'fifty times your size' which yet don't begin to have a fraction of your weight, or your character, or your intensity of presence and sweetness of tone, or your moral charm, or your pleasant appreciability, or, in short, of anything that is yours." Without "your sole and single felicity," he went on, where in the world should one have gone, "inane and unappeased, for the particular communication of which you have the secret?"[17] When he later half-humorously called Concord the American Weimar and equated Emerson and Thoreau with Goethe and Schiller, his essential referent is explicit.[18] He could nonetheless still quite beautifully understand the frustration of his father. For in James's last extended reference to Emerson, in his reaction to his father's reaction to the man, as James recorded it in his *Notes of a Son and Brother*, he described as "remarkably felicitous" his father's description of Emerson as a "man without a handle." Emerson's "great over hanging heaven of universal and ethereal answers," said James, to the "comparatively terrestrial and personal questions" of a man like his father appeared to anticipate everything except "the unaccommodating individual case."[19]

But the father's views were not those of the son. Nor was the son's perspective that of the father. It was James the artist who looked at Ralph Waldo Emerson. From his earliest impression of being in the presence of greatness through a growing critical awareness of Emerson's inability to see in the dark, the view of the son was quintessentially his own. Never blind to the limitations of the Emersonian aesthetic, as in his complaints about form and style, Henry James listened most attentively to Emerson the philosopher. Emerson's voice spoke with authority and direction only to the novelist's moral sense.

Emerson as "Sayer"

Neither Henry James the theologian nor his son the novelist, however, had the spiritual or intellectual affinity with Emerson that William James the philosopher had. Like his father and his brother, William knew Emerson personally, read his later books as they were published, and often visited the Emerson household. But unlike those two, he was unreservedly enthusiastic about Emerson's writings and was, in fact, to incorporate into his own philosophical system many Emersonian concepts—all while being aesthetically conscious of Emerson the artist.

As early as 1868, when he was only twenty-six, William suggested his own affinity when, in a letter to his brother about one of his father's more harsh diatribes against Emerson, he said, "Emerson probably has other 'intellectual offspring' than those wretched imitators" his father described and "has truly stirred up honest men who are far from advertising it by their mode of talking" (Perry, 1:270). That William himself was such a man was first comprehensively authenticated by Frederic I. Carpenter in 1929.[20] But Perry pointed out even earlier that William cited Emerson (in one of his earliest reviews) in support of his belief in "the teleological character of the mind," which Perry himself describes as "the germinal idea of James's psychology, epistemology, and philosophy of religion."[21] William himself, in his *The Will to Believe*, referred to his own early review *and* to Emerson when he quoted "Brahma" to say that "teleology (had she a voice) would exclaim with Emerson" as he had in that poem.[22]

This early, central recourse to Emerson and his concepts was to remain a constant in William's writings, for in practically every major book that he wrote Emerson was called on for illustration or support. In his first book, for example, the famous *Principles of Psychology*, he turned to and quoted Emerson to explain the fascination of metaphors, the way "'they sweetly torment us with invitations to their inaccessible homes.'"[23] He also invoked Emerson to support his conviction that "the more a conceived object *excites* us, the more reality it has": "'Our faith comes in moments. . . . Yet there is a depth in those brief moments which constrains us to ascribe more reality to them than to all other experiences.'"[24] In his *Will to Believe*, he quoted Emerson to support his pragmatic defense of free will.[25] In *Human Immortality*, in which he postulated the theory that consciousness is not necessarily self-creating, that it does not, as the idealists would have it, make itself aware of itself, it was Emersonian transcendentalism that he said "connects itself" to his own "transmission-theory."[26] Finally, in *Talks to Teachers* we come across passages so Emersonian in tone, diction, and concept that, although they are not literally his, they very well might be. Note, for example, the following, wherein William is defending the importance of allowing one's "responsive sensibilities" to function: "We are trained to see the choice, the rare, the exquisite exclusively, and to overlook the common. We are stuffed with abstract conceptions, and glib with verbalities and verbosities; and in the culture of these higher functions the peculiar sources of joy connected with our simpler functions dry up, and we grow stone-blind and insensible to life's more elementary and general goods and joys."[27]

In some ways, however, William's most suggestive "use" of Emerson was in his *Varieties of Religious Experience*. In the very act of defining "religion," for example, he utilized "Emersonian religion" to explain its rich variety. Its concept of "a divine soul of order," William explained, although never clearly distinguishable as a "duality like the eye's brilliance" or "self-conscious life" itself "like the eye's seeing," is nevertheless an "active" force, "as much as if it were a God," and "we can trust it to protect all ideal interests." That Emerson's use of the concept was determined by its ability "to suit the literary rather than the philosophic need" makes of it no less a religion than any other. But such a remark also suggests that it was the literary or artistic Emerson, rather than the philosophical one, that was beginning to interest William James. Elsewhere in this most provocative book is his attack on "*modern* transcendental idealism" (emphasis added), that "Emersonianism" that "seems to let God evaporate into abstract Ideality." Yet he could also see that it was "the essentially spiritual nature of the universe" that was "the object of the transcendentalist cult" and that "the frank expression of this worship of mere abstract laws was what made the scandal of the performance."[28] William also entered a slight demurrer to Emerson's characteristic disdain for those who "resist" their native impulses; James himself felt that some resistance to some impulses might well be well founded. Finally, in his reiterated belief that religious experience had to be individually experienced, however varied, to be meaningful, he playfully digressed into a paraphrase of Emerson in recounting some antagonisms between ritualistic minds and the "formless spaciousness" (as the ritualists might have conceived it) of transcendentalism.[29]

The intimation in this volume that it was Emerson the artist who spoke most eloquently to William James was first to be fully demonstrated in the address he was invited to deliver at the Emerson birthday centennial at Concord in 1903, the most deliberate and formal assessment of Emerson he was to make. Assiduously preparing for the occasion, he characteristically reread all of Emerson, and on 3 May he wrote his brother Henry that "the reading of the divine Emerson, volume after volume," had done him "a lot of good," had even "thrown a strong practical light" on his own "path." "The incorruptible way in which he followed his own vocation . . . , *reporting them in the right literary form*" (emphasis added), he went on, was "a moral lesson to all men who have any genius, however small, to foster."[30]

In the speech itself, after a glittering opening on the "distinction" of Emerson and the harmonious combination of his gifts, William first stressed the unfailing faithfulness with which Emerson was loyal to his own capabilities and form, his recognition of the need for the right word for the right thought. It is only when thought and expression are one, said William, that we have an artist such as Emerson, "an artist whose medium was verbal and who wrought in spiritual material" (*JF*, p. 454).

William was not blind to how Emerson's conscientious attention to the "duty of spiritual seeing and reporting" (*JF*, p. 455) would strike some as provokingly remote. At the same time, he argued, it is with Emerson that we best see that in individual fact is found universal reason. Hence, if the absolute appears out of the fact—"The fact is the sweetest dream that labor knows," as Robert Frost was still later to put it in "Mowing"[31]—there is something mandatory about assessing an original relation to the universe. Emerson's belief in the sacredness of life at first hand is thus second only to its corollary, which James called Emerson's "hottest persuasion": we should not discover truth through others' eyes. Such independence electrified Emerson's generation, said William, and was "the soul of his message." In another passage, James wrote as if he had been Emerson himself: "The present man is the aboriginal reality, the Institution is derivative, and the past man is irrelevant and obliterate for present issues" (*JF*, pp. 455–56). Emerson's independent, available, self-reliant, and thus *pragmatic* artistry was his great gift.

James was elsewhere in the address to talk of Emerson's lack of vanity and pretense, of the ways "character infallibly proclaims itself," but the need for authenticity is paramount in the indefeasible right to be exactly what one is. Optimistic sentimentality otherwise results. "Emersonian optimism," said William, "had nothing in common with that indiscriminate hurrahing for the Universe with which Walt Whitman has made us familiar." Fact and moment reveal the divine spark only when they are sincere, authentic, archetypal; when connected with the Moral Sentiment; and when symbolic of the Universe. That which fulfills these requirements is difficult to say. But Emerson, he concludes, somehow knew, could somehow see in the squalor of the individual fact its universal significance. "The point of any pen can be an epitome of reality: the commonest person's act, if genuinely activated, can lay hold on eternity . . . and it is for this truth, given to no previous *literary artist* to express in such a penetratingly persuasive tone, that posterity will reckon him a prophet" (*JF*, p. 458; emphasis added).

Most of the remainder of William's comments on Emerson stressed Emerson the artist rather than Emerson the philosopher. In 1905 in a letter to Dickinson S. Miller, for example, about Santayana's *The Life of Reason*, William paralleled and distinguished the two writers thusly: "E[merson is] receptive, expansive, as if handling life through a wide funnel with a great indraught; S[antayana] as if through a pinpoint orifice that emits his cooling spray outward over the universe like nose-disinfectant from an 'atomizer'" (*LWJ*, 2:234–35). In 1909 he wrote to W. C. Brownell that "Emerson evidently had no capacity whatever for metaphysic argument." The appeal of "certain transcendentalist and Platonic phrases" often led him, said William, to abound "in monistic metaphysical talk which the very next pages belied." Yet, he could conclude, he saw "no great harm in the literary inconsistency," for his "dogmatic expression" of monistic formulas "never led him to *suppress the facts* they ignored" (Perry, 1:144). In his very last book, *Some Problems of Philosophy*, published the year he died, he quoted Emerson in at least two instances, once to clarify a process and once to support and explicate an argument.[32]

William James was thus in possession of a somewhat more lively and penetrating insight into Emerson's significance than that demonstrated by his brother or father. The appeal to William of Emerson's independence, self-reliance, and artistic perceptiveness of the significant perhaps goes without saying. That the philosopher would see him as an artist is more speculative, as is his justification of Emerson's idealism on artistic grounds. William James, moreover, was a great utilizer of Emerson, so great in fact that were Emerson to disappear from our literary consciousness a goodly portion of his thought would survive in William's own writings.[33] Indeed, the term "Pragmatic Mysticism," first applied to Emerson's philosophy by Henry D. Gray some years ago and still current, is a term whose essence was clearly anticipated by William.[34] What William owed to Emerson's style is too obvious to be remarked upon. Ultimately, however, for William James the philosopher, it was Emerson the artist who mattered most.

The "Whole" Emerson?

The pattern of these admittedly partial views of Emerson by the elder Henry James and his two famous sons is so pat and thus so suspicious that one almost hesitates to formulate it: that to a theologian, Emerson was a divine manifestation; to an artist, primarily a moral philosopher; and to a philosopher, the supreme artist. Indeed, Emerson and the Jameses are in truth much too elusive to be locked into so inflexible a pattern. Yet, Emerson himself stated (in his essay "The Poet") that "the Universe has three children, born at one time, which reappear under different names in every system of thought, whether they be called cause, operation, and effect; or, more poetically, Jove, Pluto, Neptune; or, theologically, the Father, the Spirit, and the Son; but which we will call here the Knower, the Doer, and the Sayer. These stand respectively for the love of truth, for the love of good, and for the love of beauty. These three are equal. Each is that which he is, essentially, so that he cannot be surmounted or analyzed, and each of these three has the power of the other latent in him and his own, patent."[35] For the James family collectively, therefore, Emerson *is* seen whole. For the James family individually, he is also seen whole. Knower, Doer, and Sayer, Emerson himself tells us, "each . . . has the power of the other latent in him."

Emerson and the
James Family: 1953–1980

Curiously enough, the most extensive and suggestive attention that has appeared since the early 1950s on the subject of
Emerson and the James family is that given to the elder
Henry James. The most recent study of this James is Giles
Gunn's introduction to an extensive selection of his essays
and letters (*Henry James, Senior: A Selection of His Writings*
[Chicago: American Library Association, 1974]). Gunn cites
the following as among those who have previously attempted
to give the elder James his due: Frederick Harold Young, in
his *The Philosophy of Henry James, Sr.* (New York: Bookman
Associates, 1951); Leon Edel, in the first volume of his mam-
moth biography of the son, *The Untried Years, 1843–1870*
(New York: Lippincott, 1953); R. W. B. Lewis, in *The American
Adam* (Chicago: University of Chicago Press, 1955); Quentin
Anderson, in *The American Henry James* (New Brunswick:
Rutgers University Press, 1957); and Richard Poirier, in *A
World Elsewhere* (New York: Oxford University Press, 1966).
When these accounts are supplemented by those in two stud-
ies of Emerson, Jonathan Bishop's *Emerson on the Soul*
(Cambridge: Harvard University Press, 1964) and Edward
Wagenknecht's *Ralph Waldo Emerson: Portrait of a Balanced
Soul* (New York: Oxford University Press, 1974), by another
full-length study of the elder James that Gunn does not men-
tion, Dwight D. Hoover's *Henry James, Sr. and the Religion
of Community* (Grand Rapids: William B. Eerdmans, 1969),
and by two brief lives of the novelist son, F. W. Dupee's *Henry
James* (Garden City: Doubleday, 1956) and Bruce R. Mc-
Elderry, Jr.'s *Henry James* (New York: Twayne, 1965), the
attention to the subject of the relationship between Henry
James, Sr., and Emerson since 1950 can thus quite honestly
be said to be indeed substantial.

Even so, none of these accounts substantially alters my
views of the elder Henry James and Emerson or, in fact, sees
the distinction between the two any more lucidly than did
the son William. Collectively and selectively, however, they
give a good deal more heft to the elder James's system than it
was seen to have earlier. Again and again in these accounts
we see references to James's "Emerson" as "his fair unfallen

friend" (as in Lewis, p. 55), or as "literally an innocent" (as in Anderson, p. 21), or as "intellectually recessive" (as in Dupee, p. 12). But his attraction to the man was still seen, most eloquently perhaps by Gunn, because of his possession of a "kind of divine presence," one "so serenely composed within himself and so magnanimous and tender in his relations with others that it was all but impossible to resist being captivated by him" (p. 23).

The newer element, however, seen as early as Lewis's *American Adam* in 1955 and as recently as Gunn's account in 1974, was the affinities between the elder James and the darker romantics, Hawthorne and Melville, say, as revealed in his differences from Emerson. Lewis calls him "amazingly contemporary," "closer to us than he was to" Emerson and Thoreau (p. 56). Indeed, he sees James much closer to Hawthorne and Melville and ultimately his son the novelist (p. 62) than to his transcendentalist acquaintances, going so far in fact as to see *The Marble Faun* as in part demonstrating "in action what the elder James had argued in theory" (p. 126). After a demonstration of how the ways the elder James revealed "his relation both to Calvinism and also to his age bore a strong resemblance to . . . Herman Melville" (p. 13), Gunn is led to ask rhetorically whether "Emerson's sublime indifference to any arguments challenging his position and questioning his optimism [was not] indicative of the presence . . . of that very evil of egotism which James wanted to point out to him," all the while admitting that James was so attracted to the personality of the man that "he could not bring himself to hold Emerson in any way personally responsible for it" (p. 24). Poirier also sees ties between James and Hawthorne (pp. 111–12). Anderson pays extended attention to the likenesses and differences in James and Emerson to what he calls the "bootstrap myth" (pp. 16–21). James's writing, says McElderry, was "an intelligent attempt to add a satisfactory theory of evil to Emersonian idealism" (p. 21). Finally, Dupee neatly sums up the subject with the direct assertion that the elder James admired Emerson "as intelligently as anyone ever has" (p. 12).

Any newfound views on the attitudes of the novelist toward Emerson one would surely expect to find in Edel's five-volume biography *Henry James*, published serially between 1953 and 1972. However, the most imaginative readings of

Henry James on Emerson appear in two recent books on Emerson, Hyatt H. Waggoner's *Emerson as Poet* (Princeton: Princeton University Press, 1974) and Joel Porte's *Representative Man: Ralph Waldo Emerson in His Time* (New York: Oxford University Press, 1979). Remaining accounts of relevance to my subject are mostly those that purport to find an Emersonian residuum in James's fiction.

Citing some marginalia discovered in the novelist's copy of the Emerson-Carlyle correspondence, Edel says that a phrase of Emerson's was a possible source for *The Bostonians* (*The Middle Years*, p. 137). He also reveals that James partly rewrote ("in stronger language than was in the manuscript") one of his father's letters to Emerson (*The Master*, p. 457). Beyond these revelations, however, there is little in the copious references to the James-Emerson relation in Edel's five-volume life that was not already known. Indeed, on the subject of Henry James and Emerson, Edel is at his most telling in his extended account in *Literary Biography* (Toronto: University of Toronto Press, 1957) of how he was to compose his picture in the biography of that relationship from the discovered fact of it (pp. 99–103), especially when buttressed with the additional brief remarks in his introduction to *The American Essays of Henry James* (New York: Vintage, 1956, pp. xviii–xx).

A more suggestive if limited view of the relationship is Waggoner's repeated endorsement of the continued relevance of James's "judicial reservations" about Emerson's search for but ultimate failure to find his proper "form," a judgment made about the prose but (for Waggoner) equally relevant to and supportive of his own view of the verse (pp. 18–20, 52, 192). Even more suggestive is Porte's conviction that the complex Emerson he sees is one James himself was also always right on the edge of seeing. Thus James's sketch of Emerson, he says, "without [his] perhaps quite being aware of it," is of an "Emerson whose heroism would consist in facing, with apparent lack of drama, the 'undecorated walls' of his own denuded consciousness—stripped of tradition, religious assurance, cultural appurtenance, and the consolation of high passion" (p. 14). James ironically skirts, Porte more audaciously adds, an even more complex Emerson when he brings up—"*only* to bring up"—"'the question of [Emerson's] inner reserves and skepticisms, his secret ennuis and ironies'" (p. 14). Henry James, concludes Porte, somehow saw, or almost saw, that Emerson "'was never the man anyone took him for'" (pp. 14–15). Such heady insights, mere "adumbrations" though they are candidly said to be, are exciting indeed.

Elsewhere in this volume Porte sees some striking similarities between Emerson and James's fictional Christopher Newman (of *The American*); moreover, he describes the touristing Emerson as "one sounding more like the young Henry James than Waldo Emerson" (pp. 39, 44–46). Others, however, have more methodically explored the place of Emerson's ideas in the fiction. Earl Rovit, for example, in his "James and Emerson: The Lesson of the Master" (*American Scholar* 33 [Summer 1964]: 434–40), sees the single greatest spiritual influence on James's thinking to be that of Emerson. The thrust of George Sebohian's dissertation, "The Emersonian Idealism of Henry James" (Ohio State University, 1973) is clear enough from its title. Richard A. Hocks, in *Henry James and Pragmatistic Thought* (Chapel Hill: University of North Carolina Press, 1974), supports his extraordinarily persuasive case for the importance of Henry's essay "Is There a Life after Death?" by seeing in it "something of the same authoritative quality of mind and heart found . . . in Emerson's unforgettable 'Experience,' an essay with which it compares favorably and resembles in spirit" (pp. 217–18). We find along the way in Robert Emmet Long's *Great Succession: Henry James and the Legacy of Hawthorne* (Pittsburgh: University of Pittsburgh Press, 1979) various Jamesian characters—Sloan in "A Light Man" (p. 19), Acton's mother in "The Europeans" (p. 60), Miss Birdseye in *The Bostonians* (p. 191, fn. 14)—all *reading* Emerson. The "powerful, luminous abstraction" of Emerson became for the elder James, says McElderry, "a System. With the novelist they are concrete discoveries" (p. 159). Extensive enough, therefore, is this subsequent attention to Emerson's ideas in Henry James's writings.

Apparently because the affinities had, by the early 1950s, already been so clearly established, very little attention since then has been given to the relationship between William James and Emerson, not in the recent biographies of Emerson, in separate articles on the subject, or even in recent biographies and studies of the philosopher himself. Even Gay

Wilson Allen's *William James: A Biography* (New York: Viking Press, 1967), the standard "life," appears to take the connection more or less for granted. Although his opening sentence describes William James as America's "first renowned philosopher after Emerson" (p. vii), a judgment he is to echo near the end of the volume (p. 493), and he says that one might regard the first meeting between the two (William at the time was three months old) as "a prophetic event for the future philosopher of Pragmatism" (p. 13), he nowhere gives an extended assessment of the relationship. He does cite numerous parallels and echoes (pp. 168, 187, 376, 377, 432) and makes clear how thoroughly William knew Emerson (p. 172). Indeed, in an article he had published in 1965, "James's *Varieties of Religious Experience* as Introduction to American Transcendentalism" (*Emerson Society Quarterly*, no. 39: 81–85), he described that book as the best introduction there is to that subject.

Alfred S. Reid's misleadingly titled "Emerson and Bushnell as Forerunners of Jamesian Pragmatism" (in *Furman University Bulletin*, n.s. 13 [November 1965]: 18–30) is almost exclusively devoted to Bushnell, as Reid himself acknowledges in his remark that Emerson's role in the development of pragmatism is well known. Daniel McInerney's "Suggestions on the Theme of the One and the Many in Henry James, Senior, Ralph Waldo Emerson, and William James" (*Eros*, 7 [April 1980]: 1–17) perhaps makes fewer distinctions than it should between Emerson and the elder James in his otherwise careful tracing of what William owed to father and friend in his own conception of the problem. The single most exciting corroboration about William James's attitude toward Emerson is Jonathan Bishop's observation (in a footnote to p. 237) that the philosopher "is one of surprisingly few commentators to speak even in generalities about the intimate connection between Emerson's point and the facts of his style." This recognition of William James's interest in the *artistry* of Emerson is a conviction I of course also hold.

Some qualification is thus called for by this most recent attention to the subjects of my earliest contextual configuration. The system of the elder Henry James is much more widely known (and indeed respected) than it was, even if his basic attractions to and reservations about his friend Emerson have not been seen in substantially different ways. The attitudes of the son the novelist have struck some surprisingly responsive chords in such recent studies of Emerson the man as that by Porte and of Emerson the poet as that by Waggoner. Emersonian "ideas," moreover, are now much more pervasively seen in the fiction than they were previously. The relationship of William James and Emerson is still seen much as it was in 1953. Their *collective* view of Emerson is thus, if anything, simply seen as richer. The concept of Knower, Doer, and Sayer is comprehensive enough, to be sure, to cover a multitude of critical sins. My own view about what I concluded earlier is that I can retain some faith in its general validity, although I feel some despair in its simplifications. Still, I have at least some diffident satisfaction at where this then-unconscious method was eventually to lead me.

Notes

2. A Whale, an Heiress, and a Southern Demigod

1. For extended recent attention to this "fifth" narrator, see Susan Resneck Parr, "The Fourteenth Image of the Blackbird: Another Look at Truth in *Absalom, Absalom!*" *Arizona Quarterly* 35 (summer 1979): 153–63, and Thomas E. Connolly, "Point of View in Faulkner's *Absalom, Absalom!*" forthcoming in *Modern Fiction Studies* in 1981.

3. Benjy Compson, Jake Barnes, and Nick Carraway

1. All from Michael Millgate, *The Achievement of William Faulkner* (New York: Random House, 1966), p. 89. This account is that given at the Nagano Seminar, in Japan, in 1955.

2. For one writer's attempt at a succinct view of that larger context, see William T. Stafford, *Twentieth Century American Writing* (New York: Odyssey Press, 1965), pp. 3–5.

3. Quoted in F. O. Matthiessen, *The James Family* (New York: Knopf, 1947), pp. 441–42, 452.

4. Frederick L. Gwynn and Joseph L. Blotner, eds., *Faulkner in the University* (New York: Vintage Books, 1965), p. 1.

5. William Faulkner, *The Sound and the Fury* (New York: Modern Library, 1946), pp. 93–94. Hereafter cited as *SAF*.

6. Jean Stein, "William Faulkner: An Interview," in *William Faulkner: Criticism*, ed. Frederick J. Hoffman and Olga W. Vickery (East Lansing: Michigan State University Press, 1960), p. 73.

7. Frederick J. Hoffman, *The Twenties: American Writing in the Post-War Decade*, rev. ed. (New York: Free Press, 1964), p. 247.

8. See, for example, Olga W. Vickery, *The Novels of William Faulkner*, rev. ed. (Baton Rouge: Louisiana State University Press, 1964), pp. 28–49, and Edmond L. Volpe, *A Reader's Guide to William Faulkner* (New York: Noonday Press, 1964), pp. 87–126. For a provocative

variation, see also Laurence E. Bowling, "Faulkner and the Theme of Innocence," *Kenyon Review* 10 (summer 1958): 466–87.

9. Frederick J. Hoffman, *William Faulkner* (New York: Twayne, 1961), p. 58.

10. Millgate, for example, describes the Quentin section as "a deliberate exercise in the Joycean mode" (Millgate, *Achievement of Faulkner*, p. 100); R. P. Adams sees T. S. Eliot "especially visible in Quentin's section" (*Faulkner: Myth and Motion* [Princeton: Princeton University Press, 1968], p. 231); and Joseph W. Reed, Jr., points to Werther, Childe Harold, Trigorin (*Faulkner's Narrative* [New Haven: Yale University Press, 1973], p. 82). The Jason section has been paired with Sinclair Lewis's Babbitt and the speaking voice in *The Man Who Knew Coolidge* (Millgate, *Achievement of Faulkner*, p. 100), with the oral tradition of the Southwestern Humorists, and with others (see Adams, *Faulkner*, p. 239, and Reed, *Faulkner's Narrative*, pp. 79–80).

11. Cleanth Brooks, *William Faulkner: The Yoknapatawpha Country* (New Haven: Yale University Press, 1963), p. 326.

12. Millgate, *Achievement of Faulkner*, p. 100.

13. Reed, *Faulkner's Narrative*, p. 82.

14. Reed, *Faulkner's Narrative*, pp. 76, 78–79.

15. See Volpe, *Reader's Guide*, pp. 360–77, or Dorothy Tuck, *Crowell's Handbook of Faulkner* (New York: Thomas Y. Crowell, 1964), pp. 23–25.

16. Mark Spilka, "The Death of Love in *The Sun Also Rises*," in *Twelve Original Essays on Great American Novels*, ed. Charles Shapiro (Detroit: Wayne State University Press, 1958), pp. 238–56.

17. Ernest Hemingway, *The Sun Also Rises* (New York: Scribner's, 1926), p. 168. Hereafter cited as *SAR*.

18. Richard B. Hovey, *Hemingway: The Inward Terrain* (Seattle: University of Washington Press, 1968), p. 65.

19. Ibid., and Robert W. Stallman, "*The Sun Also Rises*—But No Bells Ring," in *The Houses That James Built* (East Lansing: Michigan State University Press, 1961), pp. 173–93.

20. Arthur Scott, "In Defense of Robert Cohn," *College English* 18 (March 1957): 309–14.

21. Spilka, "Death of Love," pp. 250–55.

22. Ibid., 251–52.

23. Hovey, *Hemingway*, p. 67.

24. Some who have include Hoffman, *Twenties*, pp. 135–43; Richard Lehan, *F. Scott Fitzgerald* (Carbondale: Southern Illinois University Press, 1966), p. 174; John F. Callahan, *The Illusions of a Nation: Myth and History in the Novels of F. Scott Fitzgerald* (Urbana: University of Illinois Press, 1972), pp. 28–61; and C. W. E. Bigsby, "The Two Identities of F. Scott Fitzgerald," in *The American*

Novel and the Nineteen Twenties, ed. Malcolm Bradbury and David Palmer (London: Edward Arnold, 1971), p. 173.

25. Hoffman, *Twenties*, p. 139.

26. F. Scott Fitzgerald, *The Great Gatsby* (New York: Scribner's, 1925), p. 74. Hereafter cited as *GG*.

27. E. C. Bufkin, "A Pattern of Parallel and Double: The Function of Myrtle in *The Great Gatsby*," *Modern Fiction Studies* 15 (Winter 1969–70): 517–24.

28. Ibid., p. 521. Nick's repeated references to Myrtle Wilson's "panting" and "tremendous vitality" (*GG*, pp. 68, 138) are the only explicit indications in the novel of Nick's somehow articulated but nowhere *valued* recognition of the visceral element in Myrtle.

29. Hoffman, *Twenties*, p. 435.

4. The Obverse Relation

1. Very close to the publication of this book I chanced upon some curiously indirect, inexplicit support for my view of Paul as a generic American. According to *Filmfacts* 16, no. 1 (1973): p. 3, Ingmar Bergman "theorized that *Tango* was really a story about two homosexuals but that Brando and Bertolucci 'got worried about the taboos' and used a girl instead of a boy in the role of the younger lover; 'If you think about it in those terms,' Bergman stated in Oui Magazine, 'the film becomes very, very interesting. Except for her breasts, that girl Maria Schneider is just like a young boy. There is much hatred of women in this film, but if you can see it as being about a man who loves a boy you can understand it. It all makes sense this way.' " Shades of Leslie Fiedler and *his* views about the homoerotic tendencies of male protagonists in American fiction (in *Love and Death in the American Novel* [1960] and elsewhere)!

2. Julian Smith's paper was delivered at the national convention of the Popular Culture Association in Indianapolis in April 1973.

5. The Black/White Continuum

1. Saul Bellow, *Mr. Sammler's Planet* (New York: Viking, 1970). Hereafter cited in the text.

2. Bernard Malamud, *The Tenants* (New York: Farrar, Straus and Giroux, 1971). Hereafter cited in the text.

3. John Updike, *Rabbit Redux* (New York: Alfred A. Knopf, 1971). Hereafter cited in the text.

4. Most flamboyantly and memorably, I suppose, by Leslie A. Fied-

ler in his *Love and Death in the American Novel* (New York: Criterion Books, 1960).

5. The equation Sammler makes here between the black pickpocket and Shula is parallel to one between Angela and the black in Ben Siegel's "Saul Bellow and Mr. Sammler: Absurd Seekers of High Qualities," in *Saul Bellow: A Collection of Critical Essays*, ed. Earl Rovit (Englewood Cliffs: Prentice-Hall, 1975), p. 131. This is the best single article I know on the novel—for its sympathetic reading of the novel as a thing-in-itself and for its carefully documented account of the variety of often silly things that have been written about it.

6. For some comments on this scene as a kind of parable of modern Israel and its relations with black Africa, see Siegel, "Saul Bellow and Mr. Sammler," p. 132, and the Irvin Stock article he cites, "Man in Culture," *Commentary* 49 (May 1970): 90.

7. Wide attention to *The Tenants* in terms of its implications as a sort of document of the Black/Jew conflict of the 1960s is perhaps most elaborately represented by Cynthia Ozick's "Literary Blacks and Jews," *Midstream* 18, no. 6 (June–July 1972): 10–24 (reprinted in *Bernard Malamud: A Collection of Critical Essays*, ed. Leslie and Joyce Field [Englewood Cliffs: Prentice-Hall, 1975], pp. 80–98). In that article the controversy between Irving Howe and Ralph Ellison is said to be replicated by Willie and Harry. Those interested in this particular issue should also see John Murray Cuddihy, "Jews, Blacks, and the Cold War at the Top," *Worldview* 15 (February 1972): 30–40, for its uncharacteristically direct approach to the conflict: "a struggle over which victim is the 'real' victim, over who (Black or Jew) is 'really,' primogeniturally, entitled to the *privilegium odiosum* of Victim" (p. 39). Finally one should also see Stuart A. Lewis, "The Jewish Author Looks at the Black," *Colorado Quarterly* 21 (1973): 318–30, for a candid account of the history of the Jew/Black antagonism in America and its ubiquitous residue in a wide number of contemporary Jewish writers. Although Lewis gives my particularized subject only minimal attention, he also finds in much contemporary Jewish fiction "analogous" parallels to Fiedler's formularization of "love between the races" in "classical American literature" (p. 326).

8. The echo of Whitman's "Song of Myself," like Harry's Jamesian counterthrusts, inevitably recalls the "redskin/paleface" tradition in American letters that Philip Rahv so aptly named.

9. A much more elaborate set of parallels between these two novels is detailed by Richard Alter in his "Updike, Malamud, and the Fire This Time," *Commentary* 54, no. 4 (October 1972): 68–74, the most impressive study I know of the black/white issue that I am concerned with in this essay.

10. Robert Detweiler, *John Updike* (New York: Twayne, 1972), p. 160.

11. Ibid., p. 163.

12. One prepublication reader of this essay asked me to consider qualifying this judgment of Skeeter in the light of the later appearance of Updike's *The Coup* (1978). But after a careful and thoughtful reading of that novel, I think it is more meaningfully read as Nabokovian "play" with point of view than with the racial issue, especially in America. For a somewhat more extended view of this Nabokovian element in the novel, see Robert Towers's review, "Updike in Africa," *New York Times Book Review*, 10 December 1978, pp. 1, 55, as reprinted in *John Updike: A Collection of Critical Essays*, ed. David Thorburn and Howard Eiland (Englewood Cliffs: Prentice-Hall, 1979), pp. 157–61.

13. That Rabbit's "need" is also reminiscent of Hawthorne's Dimmesdale in his final confrontation with Hester Prynne in *The Scarlet Letter* is only another level of enrichment to the novel's more central concern with traditional black/white pairs in the American tradition, as I have previously noted in " 'The Curious Greased Grace' of John Updike: Some of His Critics, and the American Tradition," *Journal of Modern Literature* 2 (November 1972): 569–75.

14. A third critic, Sidney Finkelstein, in "The Anti-Hero of Updike Bellow and Malamud," *American Dialogue* 7 (Spring 1972): 12–14, 30, biasedly attacks all three novels as representing "the lowest point" that the "United States novel" has reached "since the end of the anti-fascist war" (p. 12). It is not, according to Finkelstein, "simply that these eminent stylists have separately written bad books. It is that the corruptions of American imperialism, of the social effects of which they are well aware, have driven them to the wall, and instead of striking back, they have accepted this hopeless unhappiness as the eternal condition of human beings in society" (p. 14)!

15. Richard Locke, *New York Times Book Review*, 14 November 1971, p. 1.

16. Alter, "Updike, Malamud," p. 73.

17. Cuddihy, "Jews, Blacks," p. 39.

18. Alter, "Updike, Malamud," p. 73.

6. Three Applications

1. My text is the "somewhat" definitive *Billy Budd, Sailor (An Inside Narrative)*, ed. Harrison Hayford and Merton M. Sealts, Jr. (Chicago: University of Chicago Press, 1962) as reprinted in William T. Stafford, *Billy Budd and the Critics*, 2nd ed. (Belmont: Wadsworth, 1968), p. 69. Hereafter cited in the text.

2. In addition to the two editions of comment on the tale already cited, see Haskell S. Springer, *Studies in Billy Budd* (Columbus: Charles E. Merrell, 1970); Howard P. Vincent, *Twentieth Century Interpretations of "Billy Budd"* (Englewood Cliffs: Prentice-Hall,

1971); and the annual chapter on Melville in *American Literary Scholarship: An Annual*, published since 1963 by Duke University Press.

3. C. Hartley Grattan, "The Calm within the Cyclone," *Nation* 134 (17 February 1932): 203.

4. I have frequently maintained elsewhere, for example, to have seen shocking parallels in the roles played by blacks in the fiction of James Baldwin and in that of William Faulkner. This is in spite of the radical disparities in their backgrounds—one Northern metropolitan, one Southern rural and patrician. Yet, time and again in their fiction it is the American black who serves as a touchstone for their moral universes. In both writers' work it is most often the black who is said to know the most because he has suffered the most. However Jeffersonian and Emersonian that stance is, moreover, it gives scant comfort to a victim to know that the perpetration of an injustice is thought to be ultimately more damaging to the perpetrator than to the victim. But even this singularity of position would not, I think, be apparent were one to know Baldwin and Faulkner only through their public pronouncements, their letters to editors, their fugitive writings, their gossip, their non-"creative" outpourings.

5. My edition is that reprinted in *Henry James: Selected Short Stories*, ed. Quentin Anderson (New York: Rinehart Editions, 1950). Hereafter cited in the text.

6. In "James Examines Shakespeare: Notes on the Nature of Genius," *PMLA* 73 (March 1958): 123–28.

7. In addition to my own, see F. W. Dupee, *Henry James: His Life and Writings* (New York: Doubleday Anchor, 1950), p. 180; Anderson, introduction to *Henry James*, pp. ix–xiii; George Arms, "James's 'The Birthplace': Over a Pulpit-Edge," *Tennessee Studies in Literature* 8 (1963): 61–69; Morton L. Ross, "James's 'The Birthplace': A Double Turn of the Narrative Screw," *Studies in Short Fiction* 3 (1966): 321–28; James V. Holleran, "An Analysis of 'The Birthplace,'" *Papers on Language and Literature* 2 (1966): 76–80; Mildred Hartsock, "The Conceivable Child: James and the Poet," *Studies in Short Fiction* 7 (1971): 569–74; and William McMurray, "Reality in Henry James's 'The Birthplace,'" *Explicator* 35 (1976): 10–11.

8. It is B. D. Hayes, not Gedge, who says that "the play's the thing" and that the desecration of the shrine "doesn't at all affect the work" (p. 256).

9. The Hayeses offer to take Gedge "up" if, at the unknown moment of mystery at the end, Grant-Jackson puts him "down" (p. 317).

10. "Oh dear, yes—just about here," Isabel replies when she is queried by one of the Public as to whether or not it is known at exactly which spot the Poet was born, "and she must tap the place with her foot. Altered? Oh, dear, no—save in a few trifling particulars: you see the place—and isn't that just the charm of it?—quite as

He saw it" (p. 245). "The lore she *did* produce for them, the associations of the sacred spot she developed, multiplied, embroidered; the things in short she said and the stupendous way she said them!" (p. 259).

11. In the four-year span between 1975 and 1978, for example (according to the bibliographical lists in *PMLA* and *American Literary Scholarship*), thirty-four books were published on Henry James!

12. Carlos Baker, *Ernest Hemingway: A Life Story* (New York: Charles Scribner's Sons, 1969), pp. 495–503.

13. See, for example, Cleanth Brooks's recent *William Faulkner: Toward Yoknapatawpha and Beyond* (New Haven: Yale University Press, 1978), chapters 3–4 passim.

14. See the opening pages of the second essay in this collection.

15. Quoted in Michael Millgate, *The Achievement of William Faulkner* (New York: Random House, 1966), p. 89. This account is that given at the Nagano Seminar, in Japan, in 1955.

16. In *Twelve Original Essays on Great American Novels*, ed. Charles Shapiro (Detroit: Wayne State University Press, 1958), pp. 238–56.

17. "Hemingway and Fitzgerald in Sound and Fury," *Papers on Language and Literature* 2 (summer 1966): 234–42. One conjunction established by Howell I find particularly provocative. Early in *The Sun Also Rises*, Howell points out, we see Jake alone in his room at night: "Undressing, I looked at myself in the mirror of the big armoir beside the bed. . . . Of all the ways to be wounded. . . . I lay awake thinking and my mind jumping around. Then I couldn't keep away from it, and I started to think about Brett and my mind stopped jumping around and started to go in sort of smooth waves. Then all of a sudden I started to cry." The parallel in Faulkner, for Howell, is at the end of the Benjy section: "*I got undressed and looked at myself, and I began to cry. Hush, Luster said. Looking for them aint going to do no good. They're gone.* . . . Caddy held me and I could hear us all, and the darkness, and something I could smell. And then I could see the windows, where the trees were buzzing. Then the dark began to go in smooth, bright shapes, like it always does, even when Caddy says that I have been asleep." Howell sees herein a "parallel correspondence of context and action (emasculation, trauma, love, motion) and of diction and syntax ('undressed . . . looked at myself . . . I began to cry . . . to go in smooth bright shapes. . . . ')" and views it as seeming "to indicate conscious intention on Faulkner's part." He even sees Faulkner's "mistakenly referring to 'Benjamin' rather than 'Joseph' as the son of Jacob sold into Egypt" as "a deliberate attempt to make Benjamin Compson the unfavored 'son' of Jacob Barnes, who has, Brett says, 'a hell of a biblical name'" (Howell, p. 236). This no doubt pushes the purported ties too far—but perhaps not by much.

18. Although Millgate describes the Quentin section as "a deliber-

ate exercise in the Joycean mode" (p. 100), R. P. Adams sees T. S. Eliot "especially visible in Quentin's section" (*Faulkner: Myth and Motion* [Princeton: Princeton University Press, 1968], p. 82). But it is Millgate who pairs the Jason section with Lewis's Babbitt and the speaking voice of *The Man Who Knew Coolidge* (p. 100).

19. *The Twenties: American Writing in the Postwar Decade*, rev. ed. (New York: Free Press, 1964), p. 435.

20. As Faulkner subsequently becomes more explicit in his parodic allusions to writers in the 1920s (most notably to Eliot in *Pylon* and Hemingway and perhaps Sherwood Anderson in the "Wild Palms" half of *The Wild Palms*), he becomes decreasingly effective. But that vexing possibility is another question altogether—and outside the purview of this essay. Howell, whom I have already referred to so supportively in fn. 17, was later to maintain, for example, and quite persuasively, in "Hemingway, Faulkner, and 'The Bear'" (*American Literature* 52 [March 1980]: 115–26) that in *Go Down, Moses*, in the short story "Race at Morning," in *Requiem for a Nun*, and even in *A Fable*, Faulkner was "perhaps . . . taking a dig at Hemingway's fumbling in *For Whom the Bell Tolls*" on the issues of "courage" and "brotherhood." Maurice Beebe once wrote me that no one, in his view, had "dealt adequately with the way in which the 'Wild Palms' half of *The Wild Palms* is an answer to *A Farewell to Arms* and the way in which Hemingway responded to that challenge by writing *The Old Man and the Sea* as an attempt to out-do Faulkner's 'Old Man.' Similarly," Beebe continued, he has "long been convinced that the Robert Cohn of *The Sun Also Rises* owes almost as much to Fitzgerald as he does to Harold Loeb and *The Sun Also Rises* is a direct response to *The Great Gatsby*." All of which is simply to support my conviction that the Faulkner/Hemingway/Fitzgerald "connection" is indeed a "vexing" one.

7. Afterword: "Knower, Doer, and Sayer"

1. In *American Literature* 24 (January 1953):434–61.

2. In F. O. Matthiessen, *The James Family* (New York: Knopf, 1947), p. 428. Hereafter cited as *JF*.

3. The correspondence covered the years 1842–72. James's first essay on Emerson, written around 1868, was first published in the *Atlantic Monthly*, December 1904, pp. 740–45. Hereafter cited as "Emerson." His second essay, written in 1881, first appeared in *The Literary Remains of the Late Henry James* (Boston: Houghton Mifflin, 1884).

4. See, for example, William James, "Introductory Note," *Atlantic Monthly*, December 1904, p. 740; Hansell Baugh, "Emerson and the Elder Henry James," *Bookman* 68 (November 1928): 320–22; C. H.

Grattan, *The Three Jameses: A Family of Minds* (New York: Longmans, Green, 1932); Ann R. Burr, ed., *Alice James: Her Brothers, Her Journal* (New York: Dodd, Mead, 1934); Austin Warren, *The Elder Henry James* (New York: Macmillan, 1934); R. B. Perry, *The Thought and Character of William James* (Boston: Little Brown, 1935; hereafter cited as Perry); and *JF*.

5. James Elliot Cabot, *A Memoir of Ralph Waldo Emerson* (New York: Houghton Mifflin, 1887), 1:358.

6. R. L. Rusk, ed., *The Letters of Ralph Waldo Emerson* (New York: Columbia University Press, 1939), 1:xvi. Hereafter cited as Rusk.

7. F. B. Sanborn, ed., *The Familiar Letters of H. D. Thoreau* (Boston: Houghton Mifflin, 1894), p. 95.

8. William James, "Introductory Note," p. 740.

9. Warren, *Elder Henry James*, pp. 184–85.

10. For William's reaction to this letter, see Perry, 1:270.

11. James had publicly questioned Emerson's understanding of Fourier when Emerson disparaged the socialist in his lecture "Greatness" at Boston, 16 November 1868 (Perry, 1:98–99).

12. Grattan, *Three Jameses*, p. 102.

13. Henry James, *Notes of a Son and Brother* (London: Macmillan, 1914), p. 191.

14. Henry James, *Hawthorne* (London: Macmillan, 1879), pp. 84–85, 99.

15. Henry James, "The Correspondence of Carlyle and Emerson," *Century* 26 (June 1883): 265–72.

16. F. O. Matthiessen, *Henry James: The Major Phase* (New York: Oxford University Press, 1944), p. 107.

17. Henry James, *The American Scene*, ed. W. H. Auden (New York: Scribner's, 1946), p. 241.

18. Henry James, *American Scene*, p. 264.

19. Henry James, *Notes of a Son and Brother*, pp. 173–74.

20. Frederic I. Carpenter, "Points of Comparison between Emerson and William James," *New England Quarterly* 2 (July 1929): 458–74. James and Emerson had been compared before this, but only briefly, as in John Macy, *The Spirit of American Literature* (New York: Doubleday, 1908), pp. 54–55, 302.

21. R. B. Perry, ed., *Collected Essays and Reviews* [of William James] (New York: Longmans, Green, 1920), p. 43 (fn. 1).

22. Perry, *Collected Essays*, p. 62.

23. William James, *Principles of Psychology* (New York: Henry Holt, 1923), 1:582.

24. William James, *Principles of Psychology*, II:307.

25. William James, *The Will to Believe* (New York: Longmans, Green, 1897), p. 175.

26. William James, *Human Immortality* (Boston: Houghton Mifflin, 1900), p. 58 (fn. 5).

27. William James, *Talks to Teachers* (New York: Henry Holt, 1920), p. 257. For still other Emerson-like passages and correspondences, see Frederic I. Carpenter, "Points of Comparison"; Irwin Edman, "For a New World," *New Republic*, 15 February 1943, pp. 224–28; Eduard C. Lindeman, "Emerson's Pragmatic Mood," *American Scholar* 16 (Winter 1947): 57–64; and *JF*, pp. 432–33.

28. William James, *The Varieties of Religious Experience* (New York: Longmans, Green, 1902), pp. 31–34.

29. William James, *Varieties of Religious Experience*, pp. 234–35 (fn. 1).

30. *The Letters of William James*, edited by his son Henry (Boston: Little Brown, 1920), 2:196–97. Hereafter cited as *LWJ*.

31. *Selected Poems of Robert Frost* (New York: Holt, Rinehart, and Winston, 1963), p. 15.

32. William James, *Some Problems of Philosophy*, ed. H. M. Kallen and Henry James (New York: Longmans, Green, 1928), pp. 56–57, 72–73 (fn. 1).

33. For a highly significant and informative article on the marginalia and marked passages in James's copies of Emerson's books, see Frederic I. Carpenter, "William James and Emerson," *American Literature* 11 (March 1939): 39–57.

34. See Henry D. Gray, *Emerson* . . . (Stanford: Stanford University Press, 1917), p. 14, and *Memories and Studies* [of William James], edited by his son Henry (New York: Longmans, Green, 1912), p. 391 (fn. 1).

35. *The Complete Works of Ralph Waldo Emerson*, ed. E. W. Emerson (Boston: Houghton Mifflin, 1903–4), 3:6–7.

Index

Absalom, Absalom! See Faulkner, William
Adams, R. P., 152 (n. 10), 158 (n. 18)
Alger, Horatio, 14
Allen, Gay Wilson: *William James: A Biography*, 148–49
Alter, Robert, 100, 101
American, The, and *Easy Rider*, 54–59
American innocence, 29–31, 49
"Americanness" of the American novel, 13–15, 26
Anderson, Quentin: *The American Henry James*, 145, 146
Anderson, Sherwood, 158 (n. 20)
As I Lay Dying. See Faulkner, William
Autry, Gene, 68

Baird, James: *Ishmael*, 9
Baker, Sheridan: *Ernest Hemingway: An Introduction and Interpretation*, 62
Baldwin, James, 63, 156 (n. 4)
Barth, John: *The Sot-Weed Factor*, 14
Beatty, Richmond Croom, 113
Beebe, Maurice, 158 (n. 20)
Bellow, Saul, 7, 26, 75, 98, 99; *Mr. Sammler's Planet*, 8, 14, 73–74, 76–84, 85, 92, 100–101; *Henderson the Rain King*, 14
Bergman, Ingmar, 153 (n. 1)
Bertolucci, Bernardo, 7, 54, 63, 64, 65

Billy Budd, Sailor. See Melville, Herman
"Birthplace, The." *See* James, Henry
Bishop, Jonathan: *Emerson on the Soul*, 145, 149
Black/Jew relationships in America, 154 (nn. 6, 7)
Bloom, Harold: *The Anxiety of Influence*, 9; *A Map of Misreading*, 9
Booth, Wayne C.: *Critical Understanding: The Powers and Limits of Pluralism*, 10
Bradley, Sculley, 113
Brando, Marlon, 63
Britten, Benjamin, 107
Bronson, Charles, 66, 67, 69
Brown, Charles Brockden: *Arthur Mervyn*, 13
Brownell, W. C., 143
Bufkin, E. C., 47–48
Bushnell, Horace, 149
Butch Cassidy and the Sundance Kid, 65

Cabot, James Eliot: *A Memoir of Ralph Waldo Emerson*, 130, 137
Campbell, Elizabeth: "Rolling Stone Raps with Peter Fonda," 58
Canby, Henry Seidel: *Turn West, Turn East: Mark Twain and Henry James*, 53
Cardinale, Claudia, 66
Carlyle, Thomas, 131: *The Cor-*

respondence of Carlyle and
Emerson, 136
Carpenter, Frederic I., 140
Cervantes Saavedra, de Miguel:
Don Quixote, 65–66
Chapman, Robert, 107
Civil unrest in 1960s, 75–76
Connecticut Yankee, A, and
Green Hills of Africa, 59–63
Contextual method, 5–8, 10,
100–102, 105, 119–20, 126,
129, 150
Coogan's Bluff, 70
Cooper, James Fenimore, 14, 75;
Leatherstocking Tales, 13, 70
Cowley, Malcolm, 60
Coxe, Louis, 107
Critical relativism, 8–10
Cuddihy, John Murray, 101, 154
(n. 7)

Deer Hunter, The, 70
Detweiler, Robert, 93, 96
Dos Passos, John: U.S.A., 14
Dreiser, Theodore, 65; An
American Tragedy, 14, 65
Dupee, F. W.: Henry James, 145,
146

Easy Rider, 7, 14, 54, 55–59. See
also The American and Easy
Rider
Edel, Leon, 146, 147; Henry
James: The Untried Years,
1843–1870, 145; Henry James:
The Middle Years, 1882–1895,
147; Henry James: The Mas-
ter, 1901–1916, 147; Literary
Biography, 147; The American
Essays of Henry James, 147
Elam, Jack, 66
Eliot, T. S., 121, 122, 158 (n. 18),
158 (n. 20); The Waste Land,
37, 120
Ellison, Ralph, 154 (n. 7)

Emerson, Ralph Waldo, 5, 6, 30,
129; Henry James, Sr., on,
130–35; English Traits, 133;
Representative Men, 133; Society and Solitude, 133; Henry
James on, 135–39, 146–48;
The Correspondence of Carlyle
and Emerson, 136; William
James on, 139–44, 148–49;
"Brahma," 140; "The Poet,"
144

Faulkner, William, 8, 14, 30, 75,
94, 105, 156 (n. 4); Absalom,
Absalom!, 6, 15, 22–25, 26, 58;
As I Lay Dying, 6, 8, 120,
123–25, 126; The Reivers, 6;
The Sound and the Fury, 7, 8,
29, 31–37, 49, 50, 94, 120,
121–23, 125, 126, 157 (n. 17),
157–58 (n. 18); Light in August, 8, 120, 125–26; Go Down,
Moses, 102, 158 (n. 20); Intruder in the Dust, 102; Soldier's Pay, 120, 122; Mosquitoes, 120; Flags in the Dust
(Sartoris), 120–21, 122; relations with other American authors, 158 (n. 20); Pylon, 158
(n. 20); The Wild Palms, 158
(n. 20); "The Bear," 158 (n. 20);
"Race at Morning," 158 (n. 20);
Requiem for a Nun, 158 (n. 20)
Ferzetti, Gabriele, 66
Fiedler, Leslie, 13, 153 (n. 1),
154 (n. 7)
Film and fiction, 7
Fitzgerald, F. Scott, 30, 48–49,
63, 65, 157 (n. 17), 158 (n. 20);
The Great Gatsby, 7, 14, 30,
43–50, 58–59, 65, 122–23, 158
(n. 20)
Foley, Mary, 108
Fonda, Henry, 66, 67, 69
Fonda, Peter, 54; See also

Campbell, Elizabeth
Ford, John, 68; *The Iron Horse*,
  68
Forster, E. M., 107
Fourier, François, 132, 134
Freeman, F. Barron, 113
Frost, Robert, 142; "Stopping by
  Woods," 9; "Mowing," 142
Fuller, Margaret, 131

Goethe, Johann Wolfgang von,
  139
Grattan, C. Hartley, 114
Great Gatsby, The. See
  Fitzgerald, F. Scott
Green Berets, The, 70
Gunn, Giles: *Henry James,
  Senior: A Selection of His
  Writings*, 145, 146

Hawthorne, Nathaniel, 136, 146;
  The Scarlet Letter, 13, 30, 155
  (n. 13); *The Marble Faun*, 146
Hayford, Harrison, and Sealts,
  Merton M., Jr.: *Billy Budd,
  Sailor*, 113–14
Hemingway, Ernest, 30–42, 54,
  63, 65, 70, 119–20, 122–23,
  126, 158 (n. 20); *The Sun Also
  Rises*, 7, 29, 37–42, 49, 50, 120,
  121, 122, 157 (n. 17), 158 (n.
  20); *Green Hills of Africa*, 7,
  60–62; *The Nick Adams
  Stories*, 42; *A Farewell to
  Arms*, 42, 120, 158 (n. 20); *A
  Moveable Feast*, 60; *Death in
  the Afternoon*, 60; *For Whom
  the Bell Tolls*, 65, 158 (n. 20);
  The Old Man and the Sea, 158
  (n. 20)
Hocks, Richard A.: *Henry James
  and Pragmatistic Thought*,
  148
Hoffman, Frederick J., 33, 49,
  123

Hoover, Dwight D.: *Henry
  James, Sr. and the Religion of
  Community*, 145
Hopper, Dennis, 7, 54, 58, 70
Hovey, Richard, 38, 41
Howe, Irving, 154 (n. 7)
Howell, John M., 122, 157 (n.
  17), 158 (n. 20)

Irving, Washington: "Rip Van
  Winkle," 14

James, Henry, 5, 8, 14, 23, 30,
  63, 70, 129, 140, 142, 143,
  149–50; *The Wings of the
  Dove*, 6, 15, 19–22, 26; *The
  American*, 6, 7, 53, 54, 55, 56,
  58, 65, 148; *What Maisie
  Knew*, 6, 99; "The Birthplace,"
  8, 105, 114–19; *The Ambas-
  sadors*, 20, 63; *The Golden
  Bowl*, 20; *The American Scene*,
  25, 138; *Daisy Miller*, 53, 65;
  The Portrait of a Lady, 65; on
  Emerson, 135–39, 146–48;
  Notes of a Son and Brother,
  139; *The Bostonians*, 147, 148;
  "Is There a Life after Death?"
  148; "A Light Man," 148; "The
  Europeans," 148
James, Henry, Sr., 5, 129, 136,
  138, 139, 140, 143, 149; on
  Emerson, 130–35, 145–46;
  Moralism and Christianity,
  132; *The Literary Remains of
  the Late Henry James*, 134
James, William, 5, 129, 132, 133,
  134, 145, 150; on Emerson,
  139–44, 148–49; *The Will to
  Believe*, 140; *Principles of Psychology*, 140; *Human Immortality*, 140; *Talks to Teachers*,
  140; *Varieties of Religious Experience*, 141, 149; *Some
  Problems of Philosophy*, 143

James family, 5, 6, 129, 144, 145, 149–50

Joyce, James, 121; *Ulysses*, 124, 125

Kurosawa, Akira, 66

Last Tango in Paris, 7, 54, 63–65

Lawrence, D. H.: *Studies in Classic American Literature*, 13, 61

Lazare, Veronica, 64

Leaud, Jean-Pierre, 64

Leone, Sergio, 7, 54, 63, 65, 66, 68, 70

Lewis, R. W. B.: *The American Adam*, 31, 145–46

Lewis, Sinclair, 121, 122; *Babbitt*, 158 (n. 18); *The Man Who Knew Coolidge*, 158 (n. 18)

Lewis, Stuart, 154 (n. 7)

Light in August. See Faulkner, William

Locke, Richard, 100

Loeb, Harold, 158 (n. 20)

Long, E. Hudson, 113

Long, Robert Emmet: *Great Succession: Henry James and the Legacy of Hawthorne*, 148

McCloud, 70

McElderry, Bruce R., Jr.: *Henry James*, 145, 146, 148

McInerney, Daniel, 149

Mailer, Norman: *An American Dream*, 92, 100

Malamud, Bernard, 7, 75, 98, 99; *The Tenants*, 8, 14, 26, 74–75, 85–91, 92, 100–101, 154 (n. 7)

Marx, Leo: *The Machine in the Garden*, 31

Matthiessen, F. O., 129, 134, 138

Melville, Herman, 8, 14, 146; *Moby-Dick*, 6, 15–19, 22, 23, 26, 63; *Typee*, 6, 30; *Billy Budd*, 6, 8, 30, 105–14; *Benito Cereno*, 102

Midnight Cowboy, 70

Miller, Dickinson S., 143

Miller, James E., Jr.: *Theory of Fiction: Henry James*, 114

Millgate, Michael, 29, 34, 122, 152 (n. 10), 158 (n. 18)

Moby-Dick. See Melville, Herman

Morricone, Ennio, 68

Morris, Wright, 25

Mr. Sammler's Planet. See Bellow, Saul

Nabokov, Vladimir: *Lolita*, 99, 155 (n. 12)

Nicholson, Jack, 57

Old-fashioned American novels, 100–102

Once upon a Time in the West, 7, 54, 63, 65–70

Ozick, Cynthia, 154 (n. 7)

Peckinpah, Sam, 70

Perry, R. B., 130, 131, 132, 133, 134, 140, 143

Poirier, Richard: *A World Elsewhere*, 145, 146

Porte, Joel: *Representative Man: Ralph Waldo Emerson in His Time*, 147–48, 150

Pound, Ezra: "Hugh Selwyn Mauberly," 37

Prophetic novels, 26

Rabbit Redux. See Updike, John

Racial unrest in America, 75–76, 90–91, 100–102

Rahv, Philip, 91, 154 (n. 8)

Reed, Joseph W., Jr., 34–35, 152 (n. 10)

Reid, Alfred S., 149

Ritter, Tex, 68

Robards, Jason, 66
Roth, Philip: *Portnoy's Com-
    plaint*, 14
Rourke, Constance: *American
    Humor: A Study of the Na-
    tional Character*, 56
Rovit, Earl, 148
Rusk, Ralph Leslie, 130, 131

Salinger, J. D.: *The Catcher in
    the Rye*, 14
Santayana, George: *The Life of
    Reason*, 143
Schiller, Friederich von, 139
Schneider, Maria, 63
Scott, Arthur, 39
Sealts, Merton M., Jr. *See*
    Hayford, Harrison
Sebohian, George, 148
Shakespeare, William: *The
    Tempest*, 115
Siegel, Ben, 154 (n. 5)
Smith, Julian, 68, 70
Sound and the Fury, The. See
    Faulkner, William
Southern, Terry, 58
Spilka, Mark, 38, 39, 40, 122
Stein, Jean, 32
Stephens, Robert: *Hemingway's
    Nonfiction*, 60, 61, 63
Stern, Milton R., 113–14
Straw Dogs, 70
Strode, Woody, 66
Sun Also Rises, The. See
    Hemingway, Ernest
Swedenborg, Emanuel, 132

Taxi Driver, 70
Tenants, The. See Malamud,
    Bernard

Thoreau, Henry David, 13–14,
    131, 139, 146
Towers, Robert, 155 (n. 12)
Treeman, Elizabeth, 113
Twain, Mark, 54, 63, 65, 70; *A
    Connecticut Yankee in King
    Arthur's Court*, 7, 59–60, 65;
    *Adventures of Huckleberry
    Finn*, 14, 94, 102; *The Inno-
    cents Abroad*, 30, 53

Updike, John, 7, 26, 75; *Rabbit
    Redux*, 8, 14, 75, 91–100,
    100–101, 155 (n. 13); *Rabbit,
    Run*, 92–93; *Bech: A Book*, 96;
    The Coup, 96, 155 (n. 12)
Ustinov, Peter, 107

Wagenknecht, Edward: *Ralph
    Waldo Emerson: Portrait of a
    Balanced Soul*, 145
Waggoner, Hyatt H.: *Emerson as
    Poet*, 147, 150
Wayne, John, 70
Weaver, Raymond, 113–14
Western films, 53–54
Whitman, Walt, 143; *Song of
    Myself*, 14; "Passage to India,"
    53
Wings of the Dove, The. See
    James, Henry
Wolfe, Thomas, 14
Wylie, Philip: *Generation of Vi-
    pers*, 14

Young, Frederick Harold: *The
    Philosophy of Henry James,
    Sr.*, 145
Young, James Dean, 16